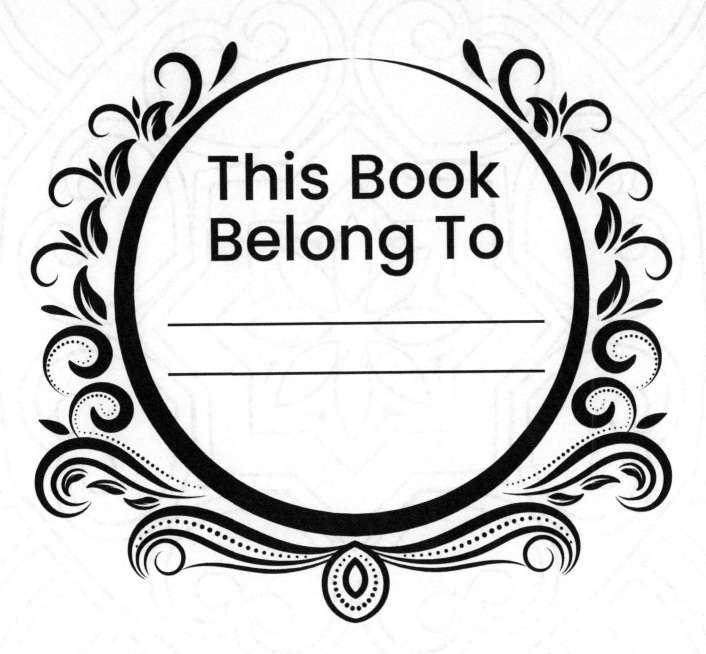

This Book
Belong To

_____

_____

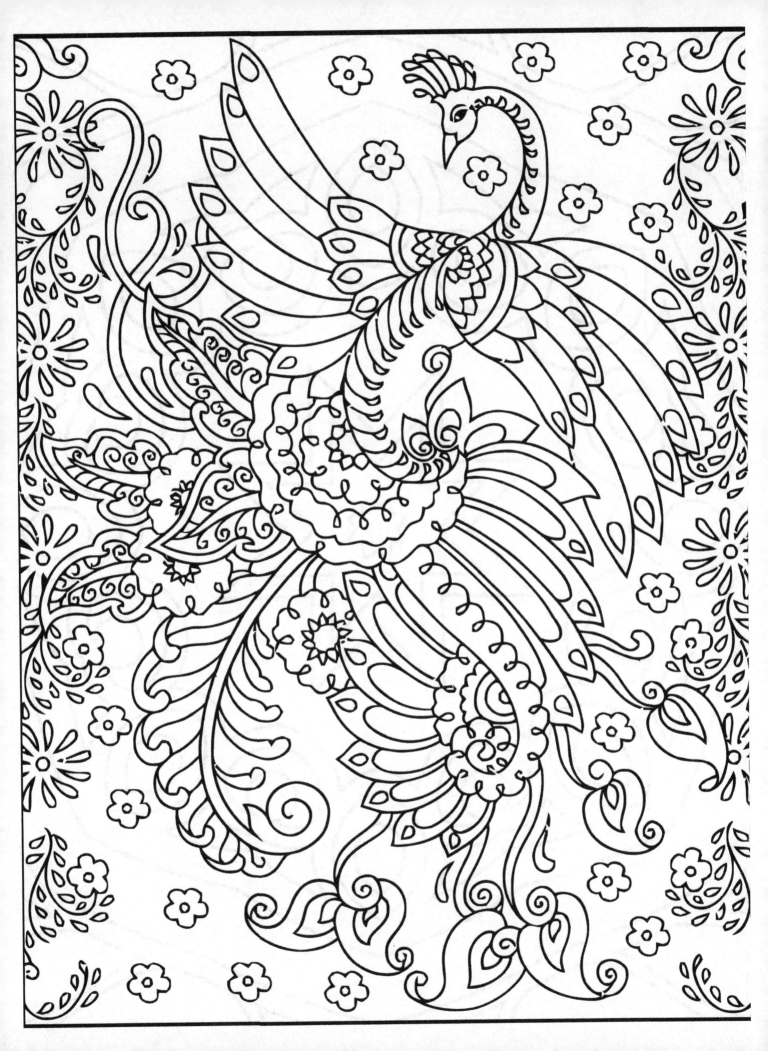

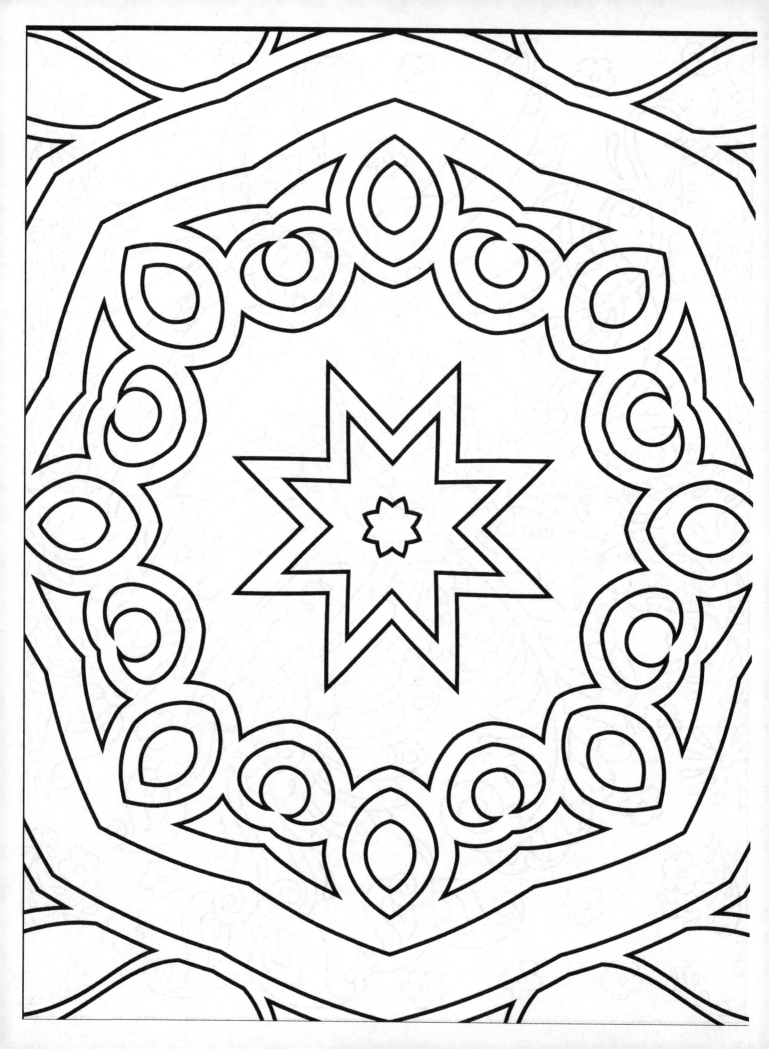

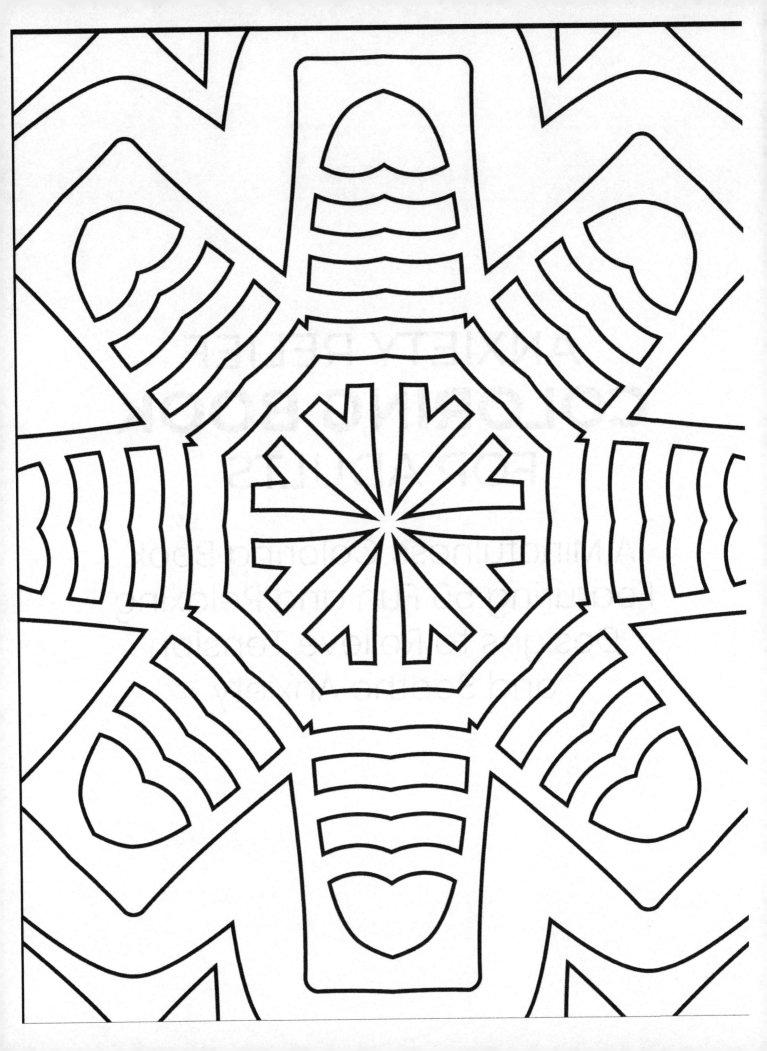

ANXIETY RELIEF
COLORING BOOK
FOR ADULTS

A Mindfulness Coloring Book
Featuring 50 Fun and Relaxing
Designs to Relieve Tension
and Soothe Anxiety

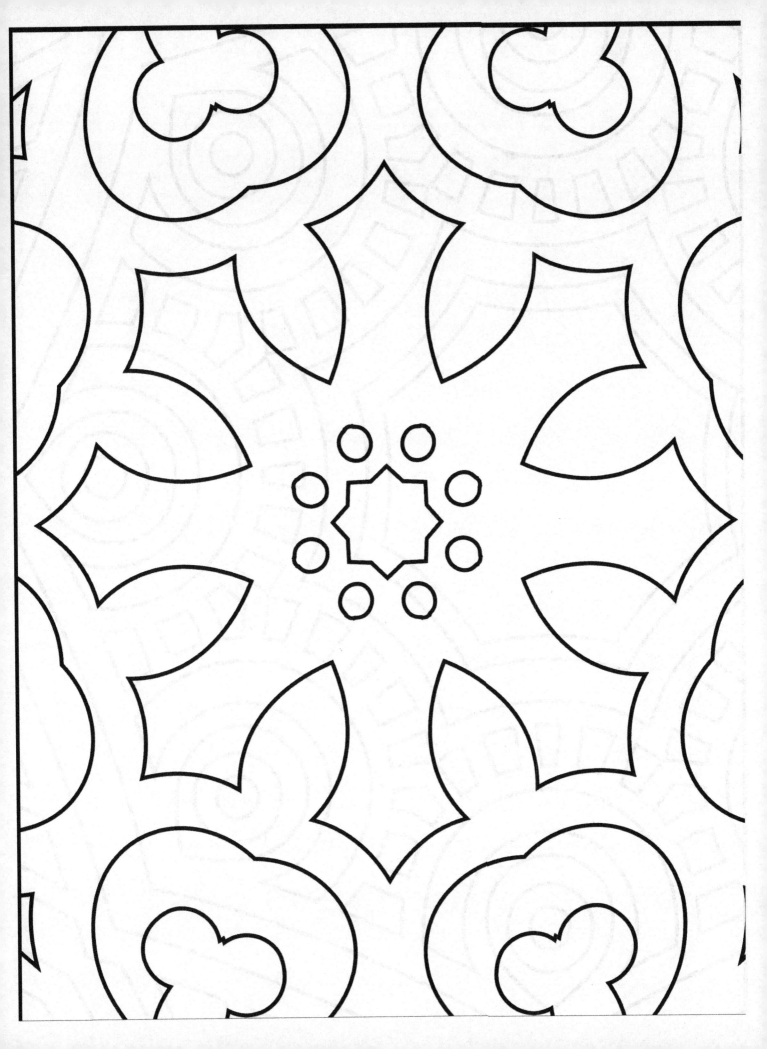

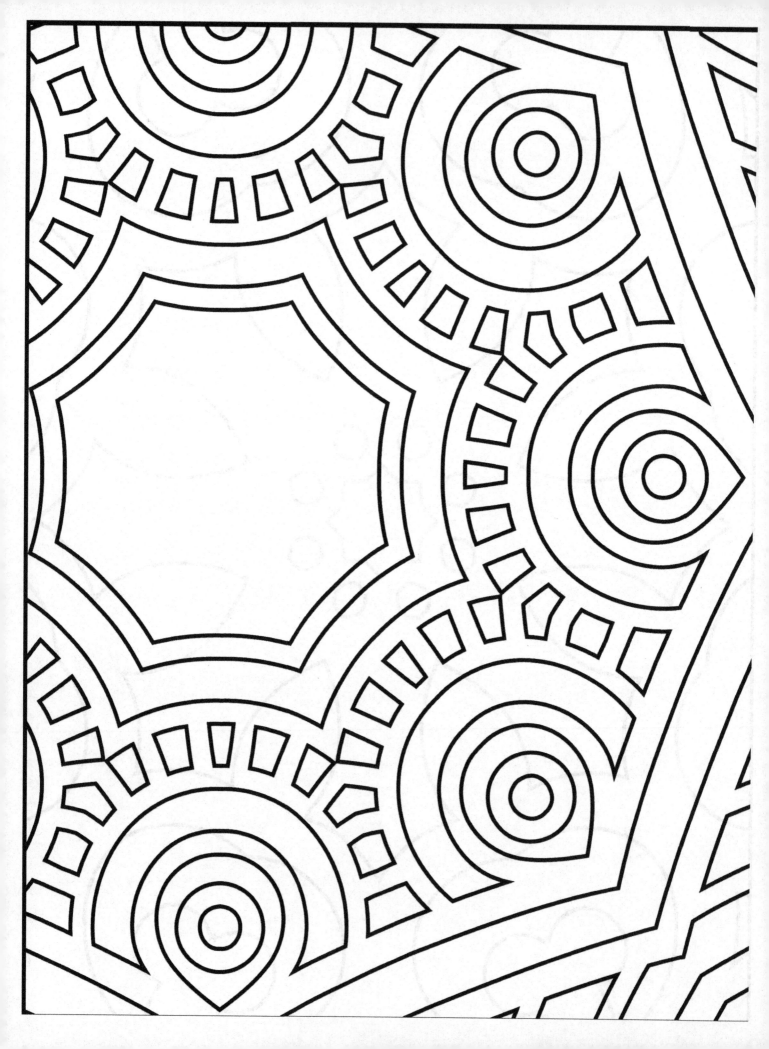

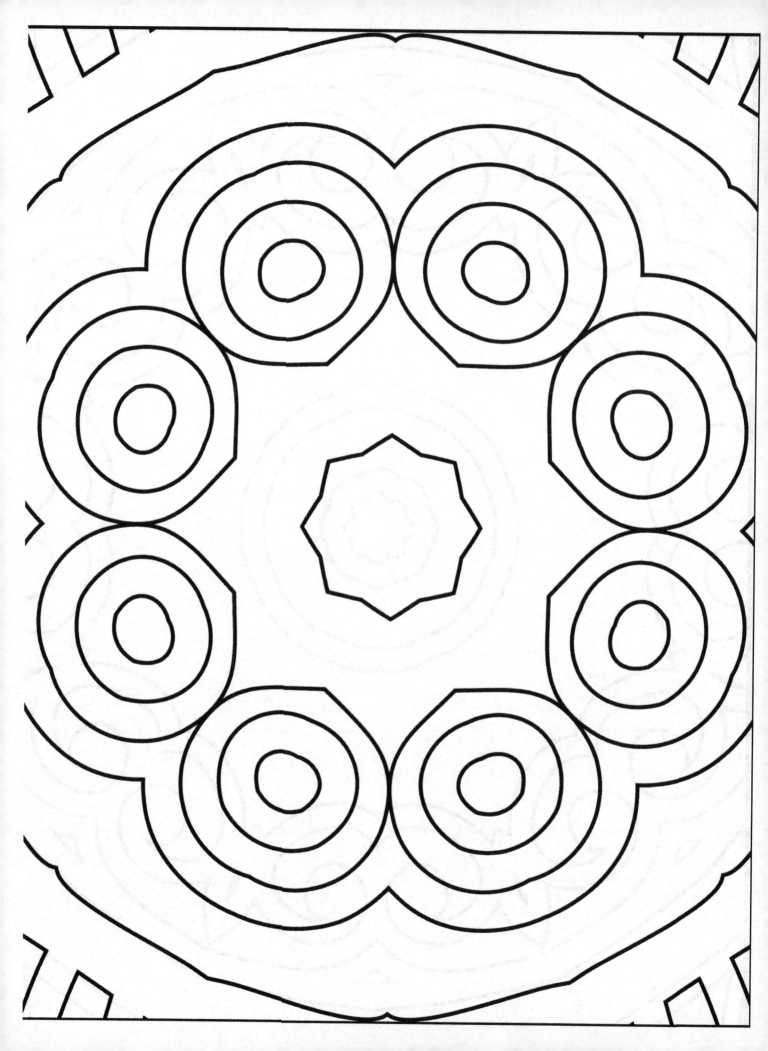

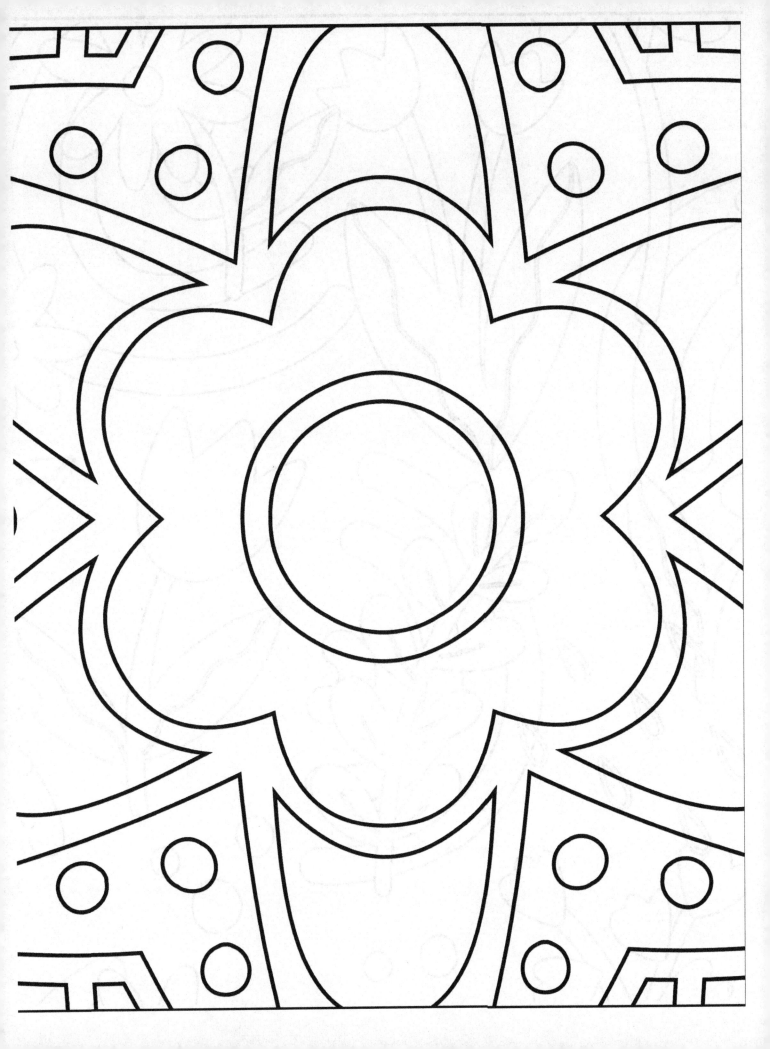

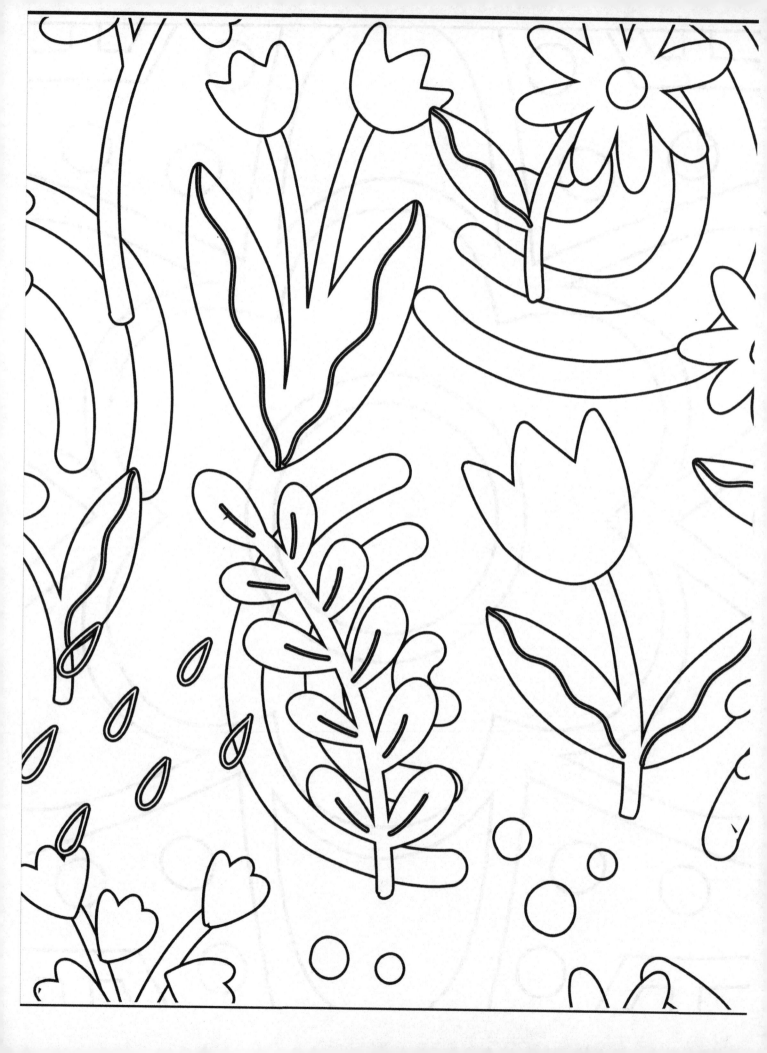

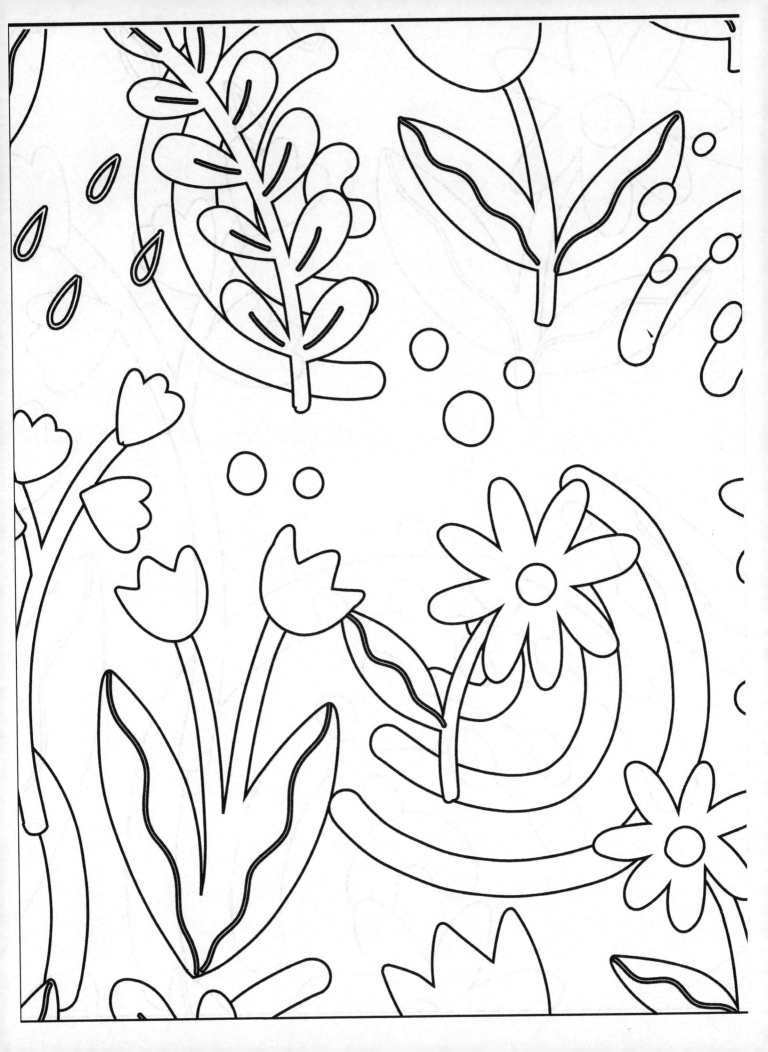

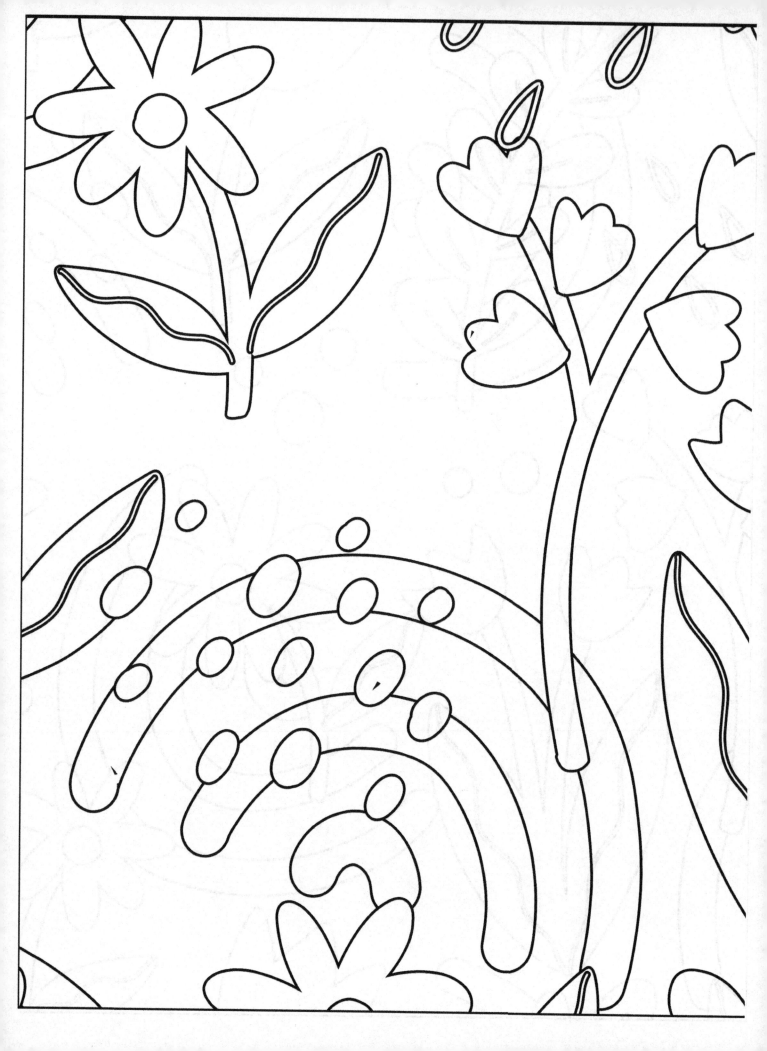

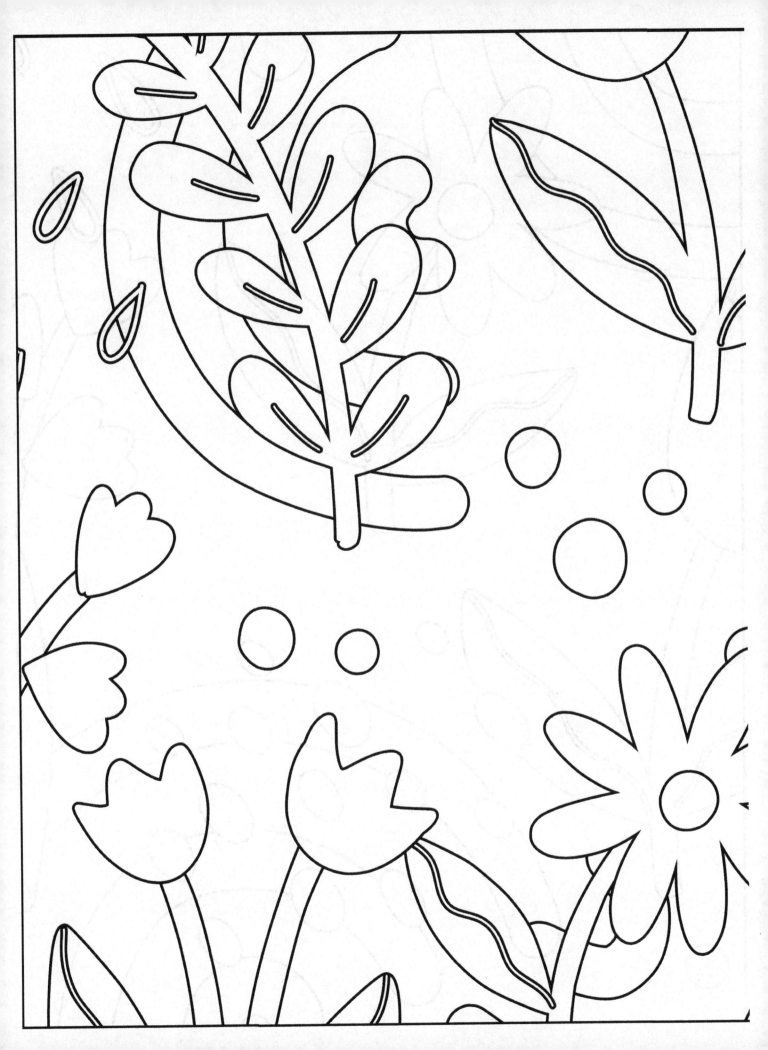

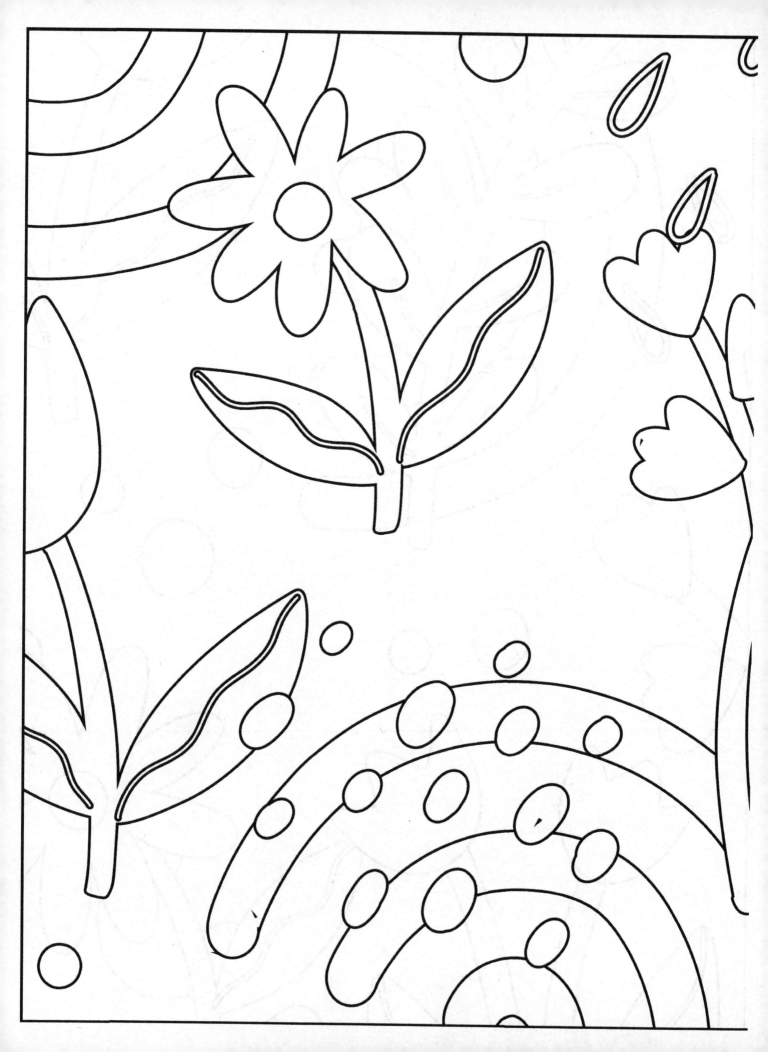

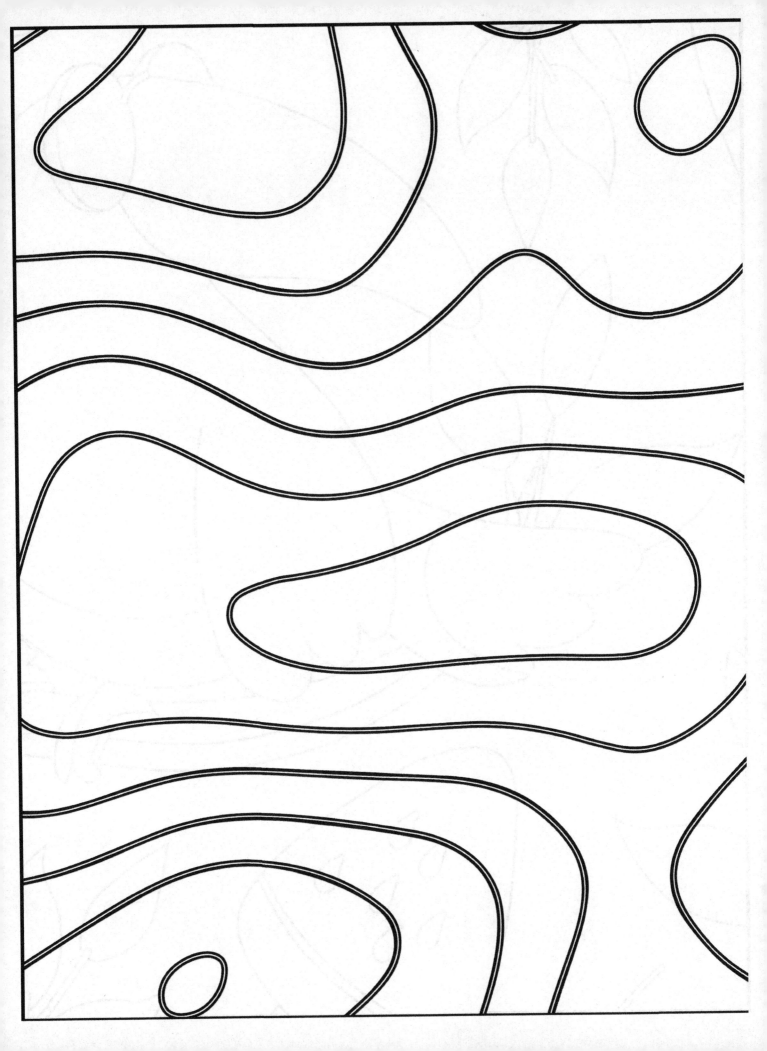

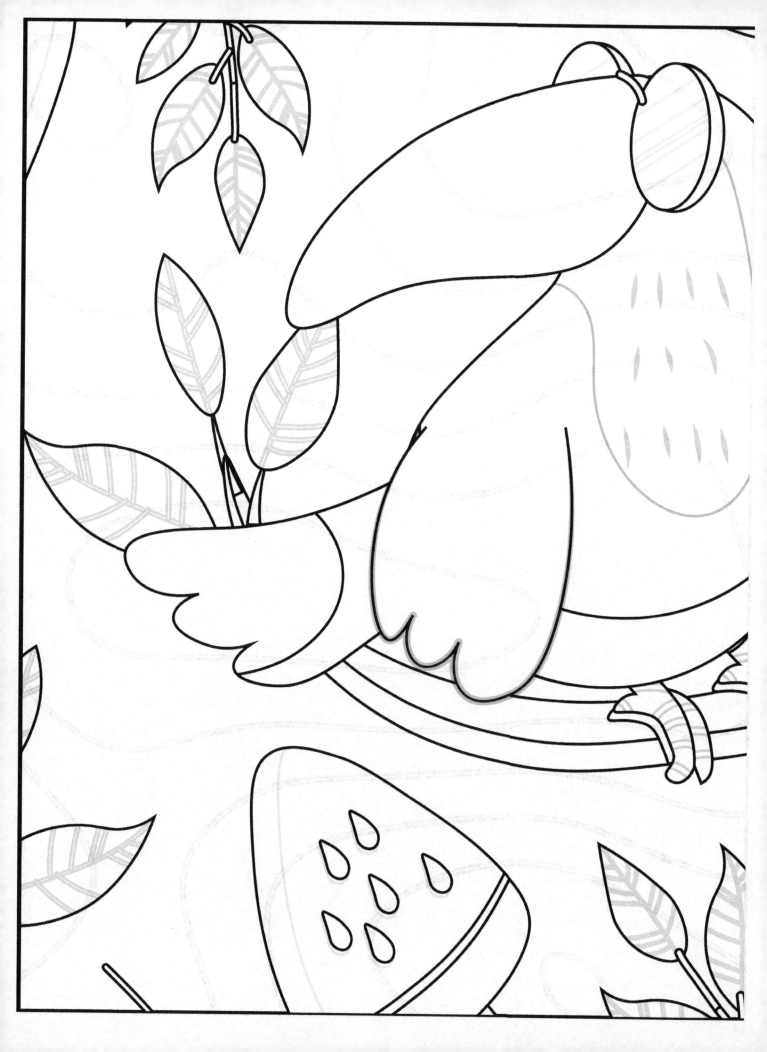

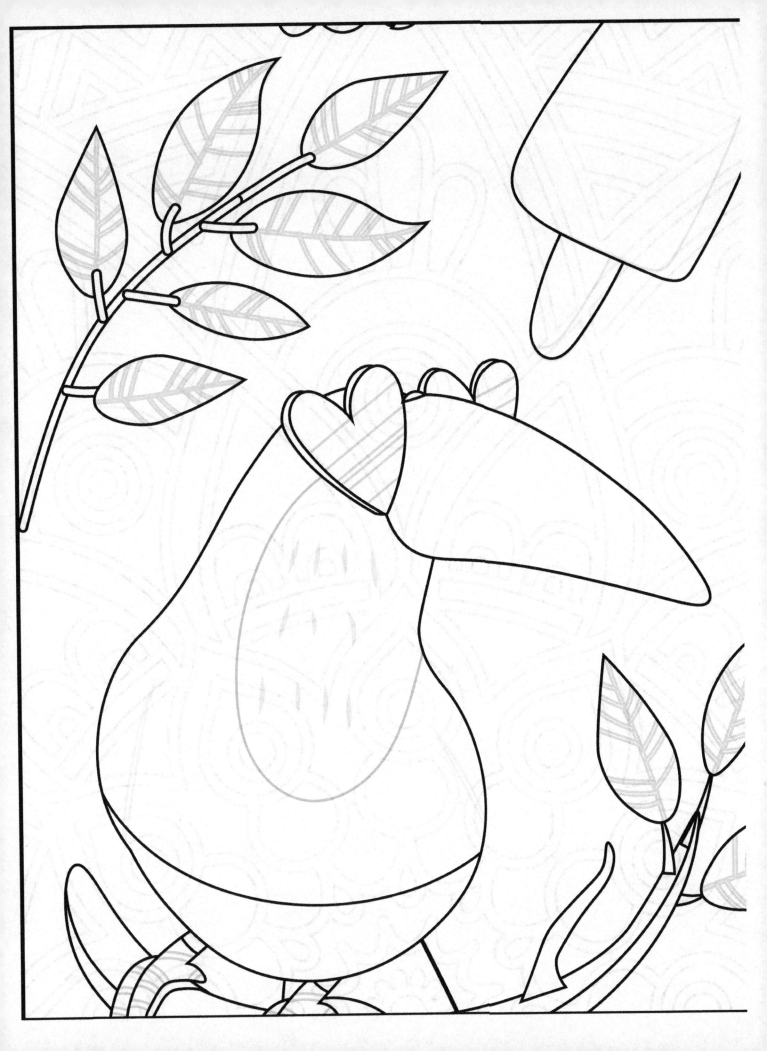

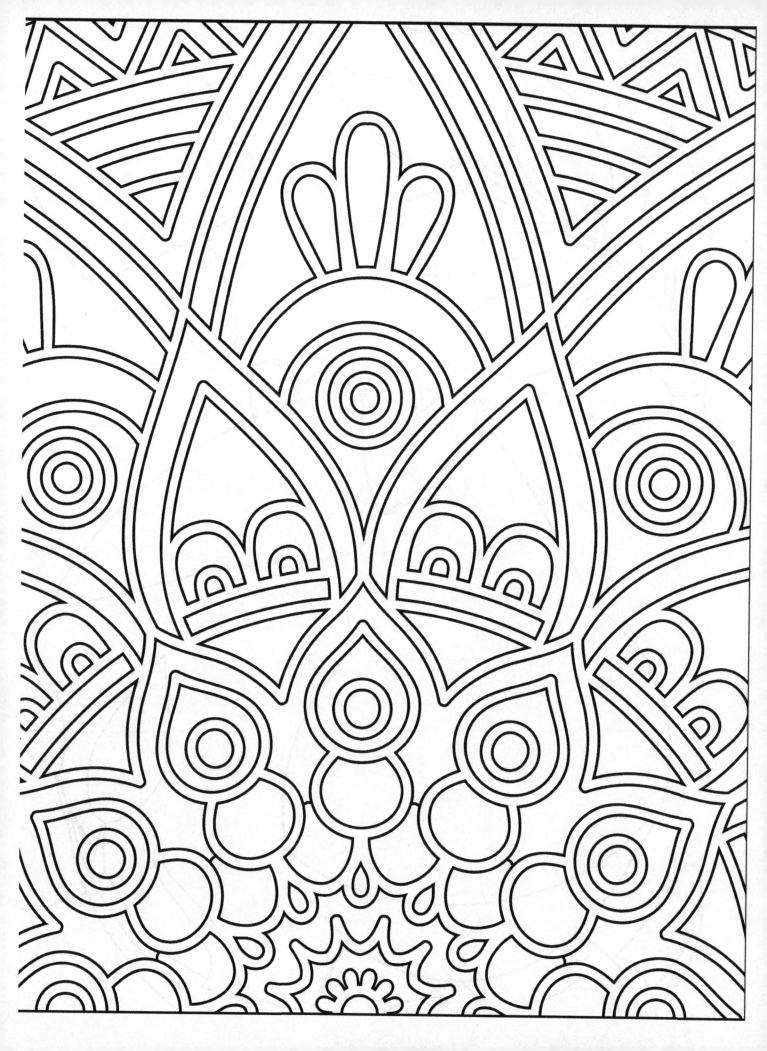

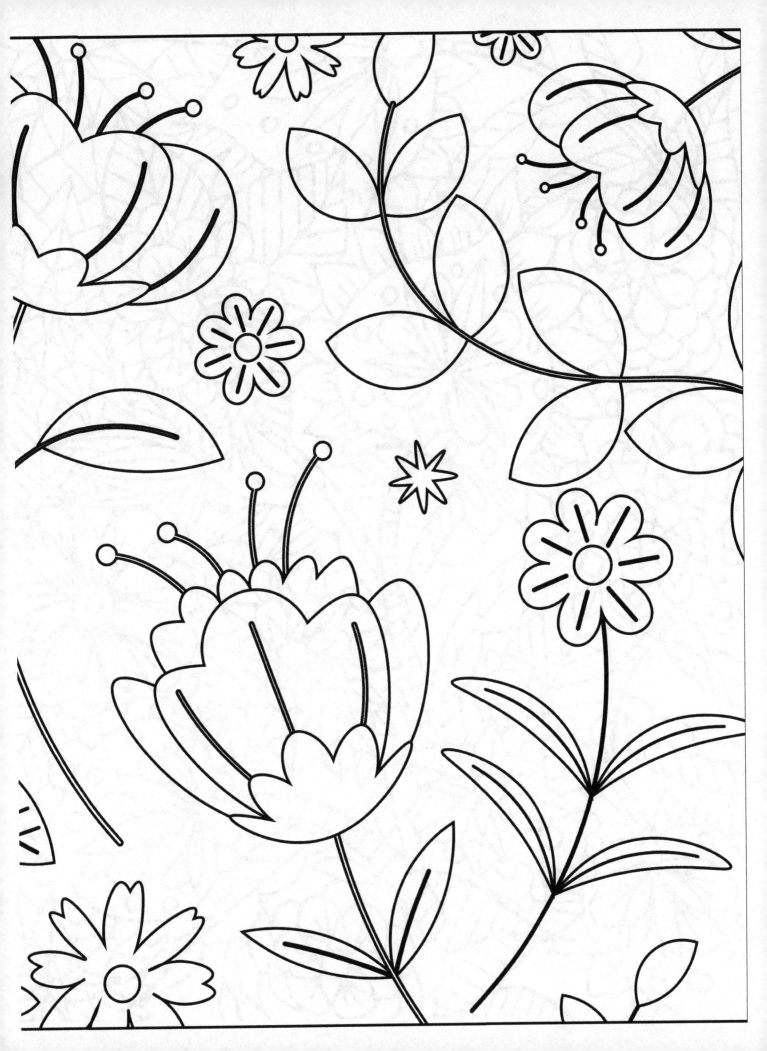

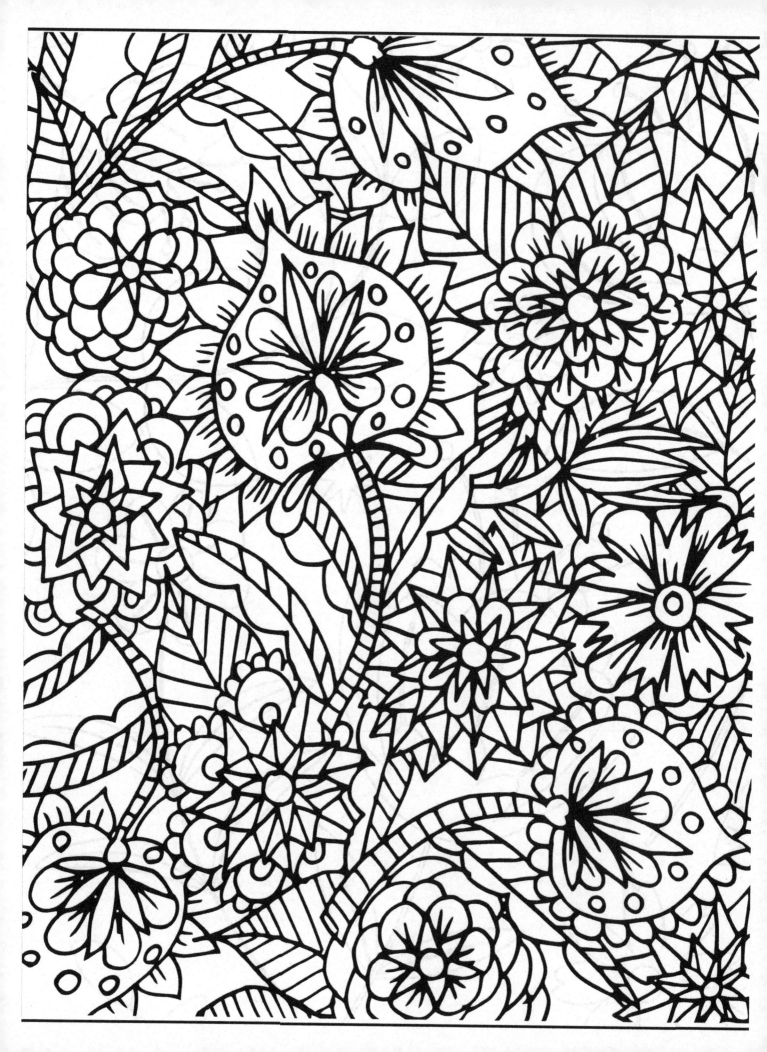

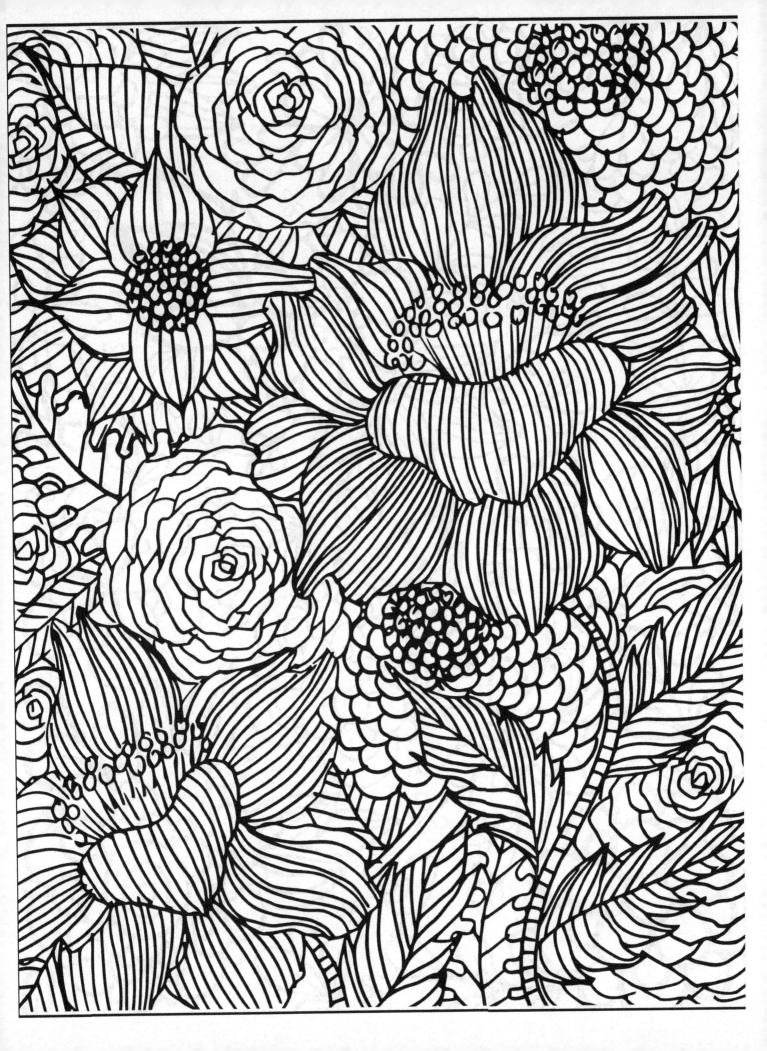

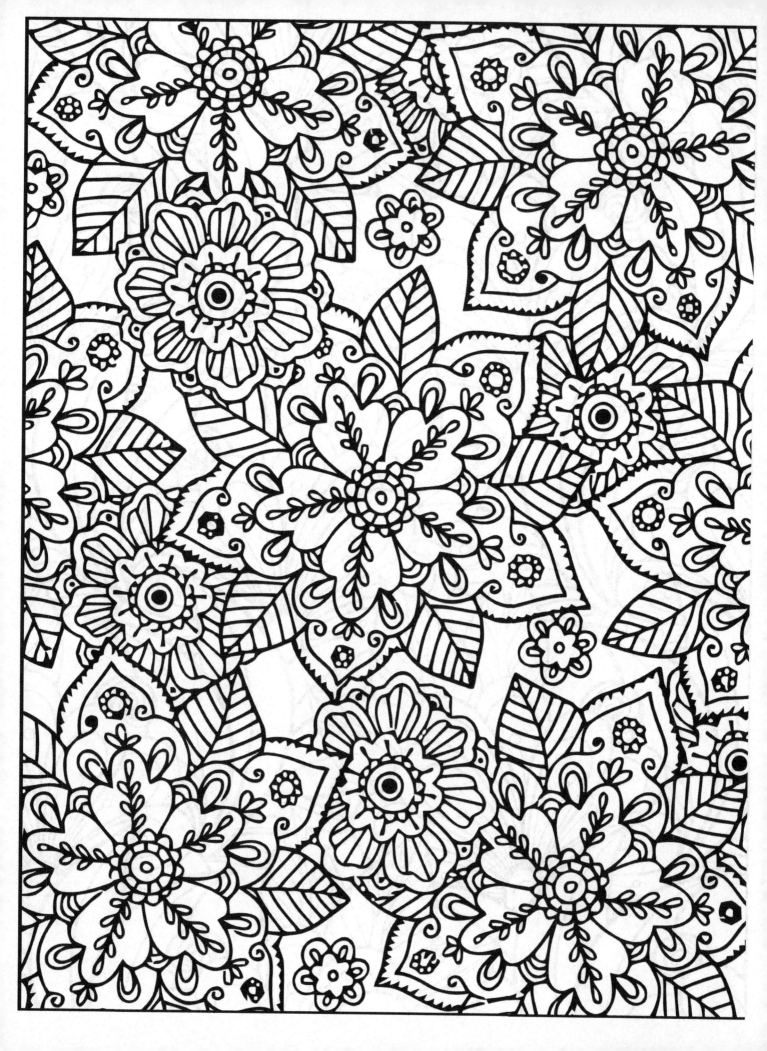

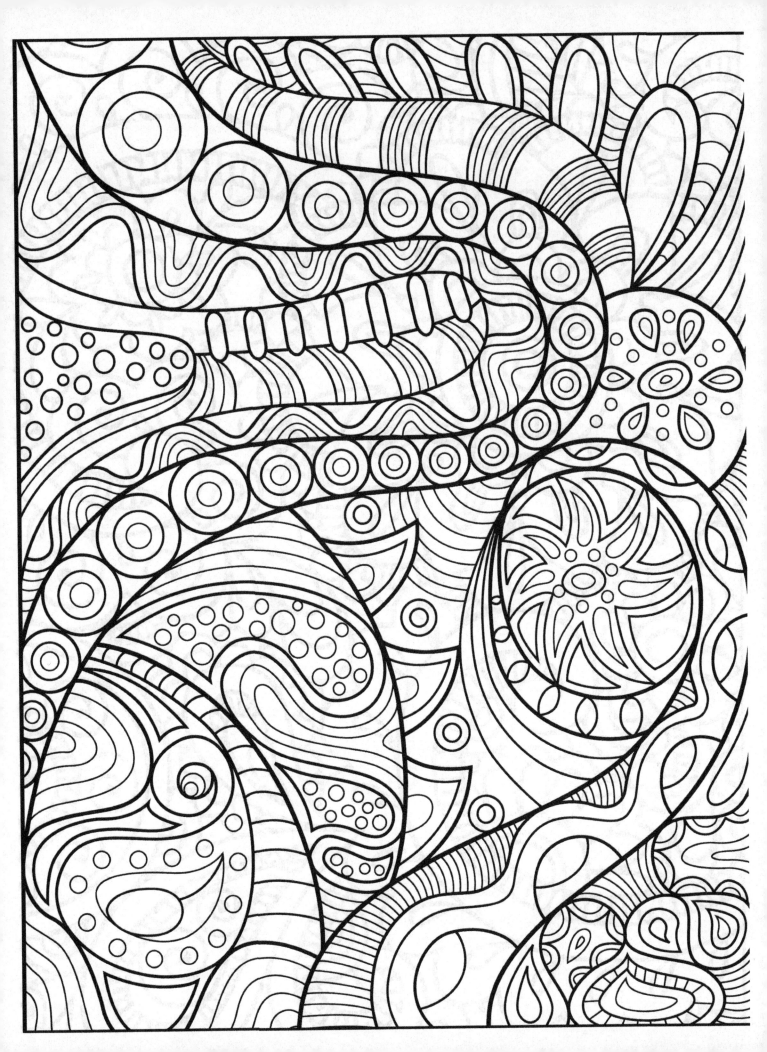

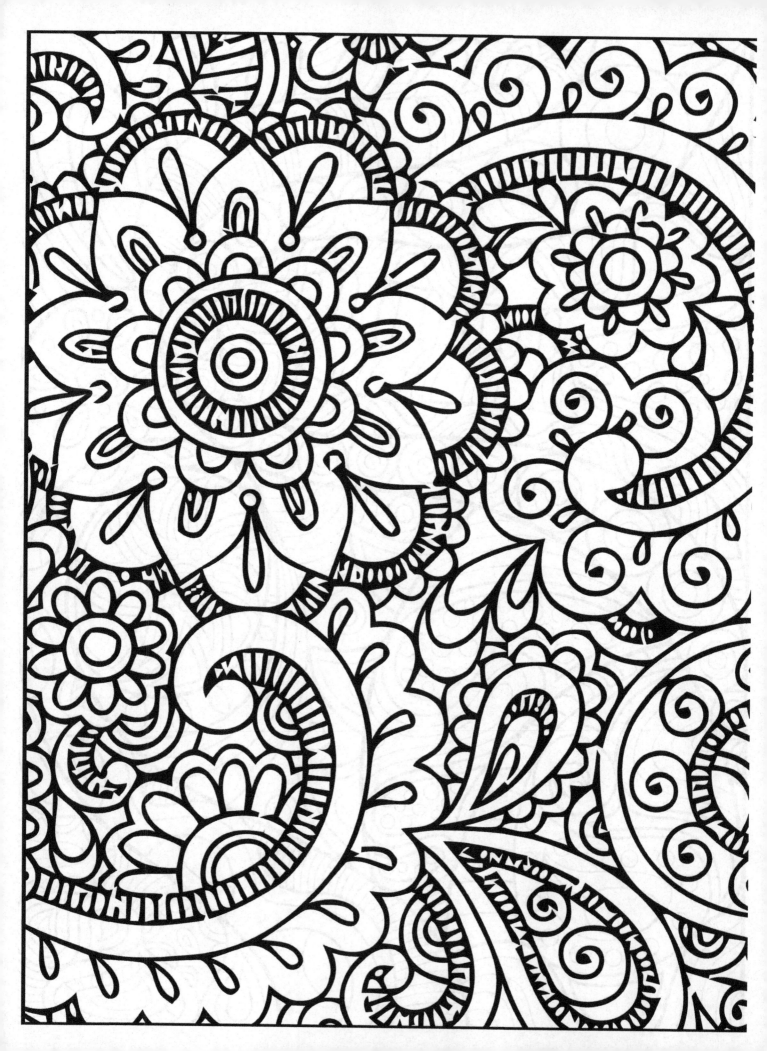

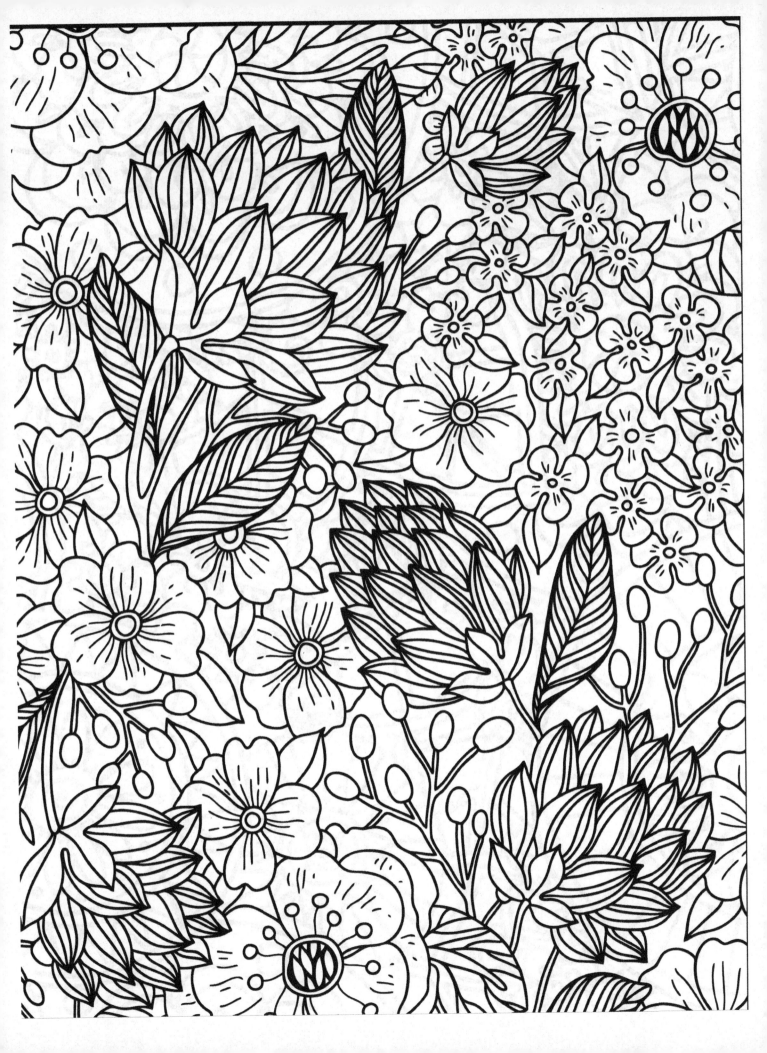

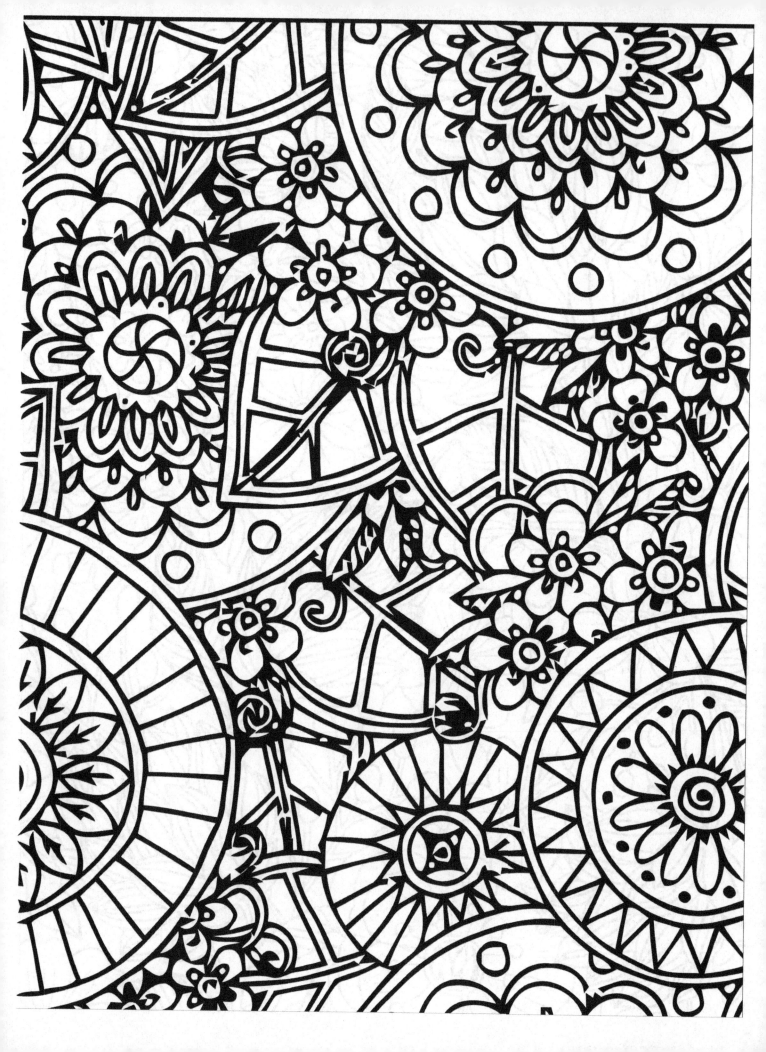

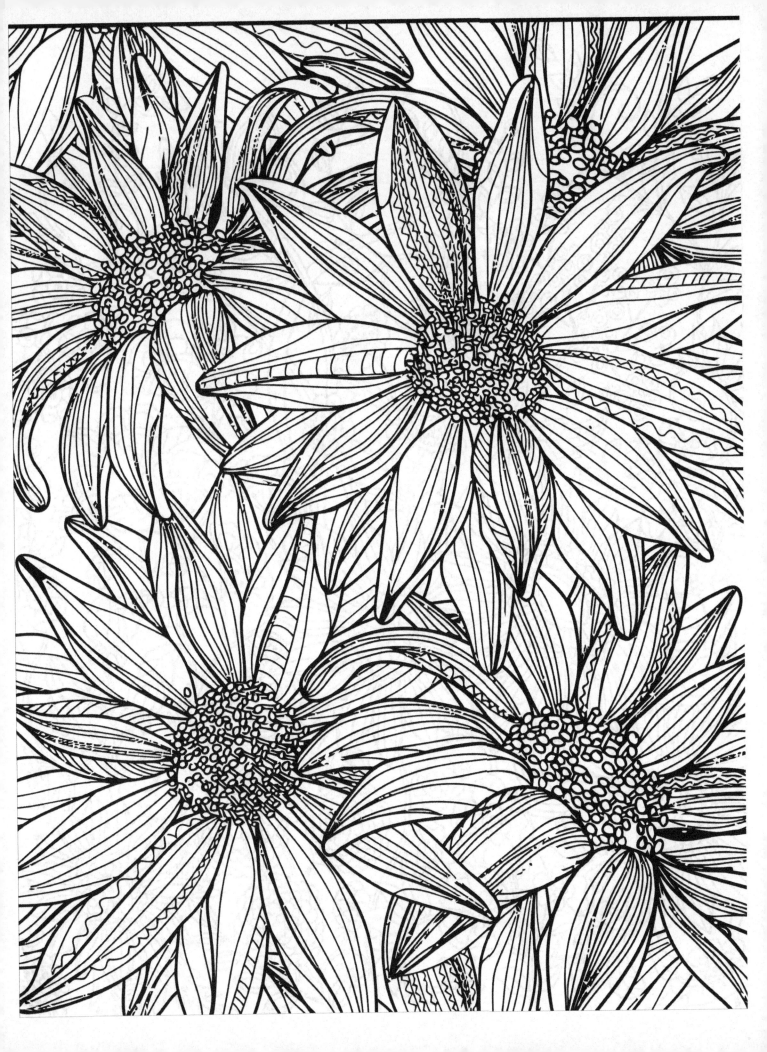

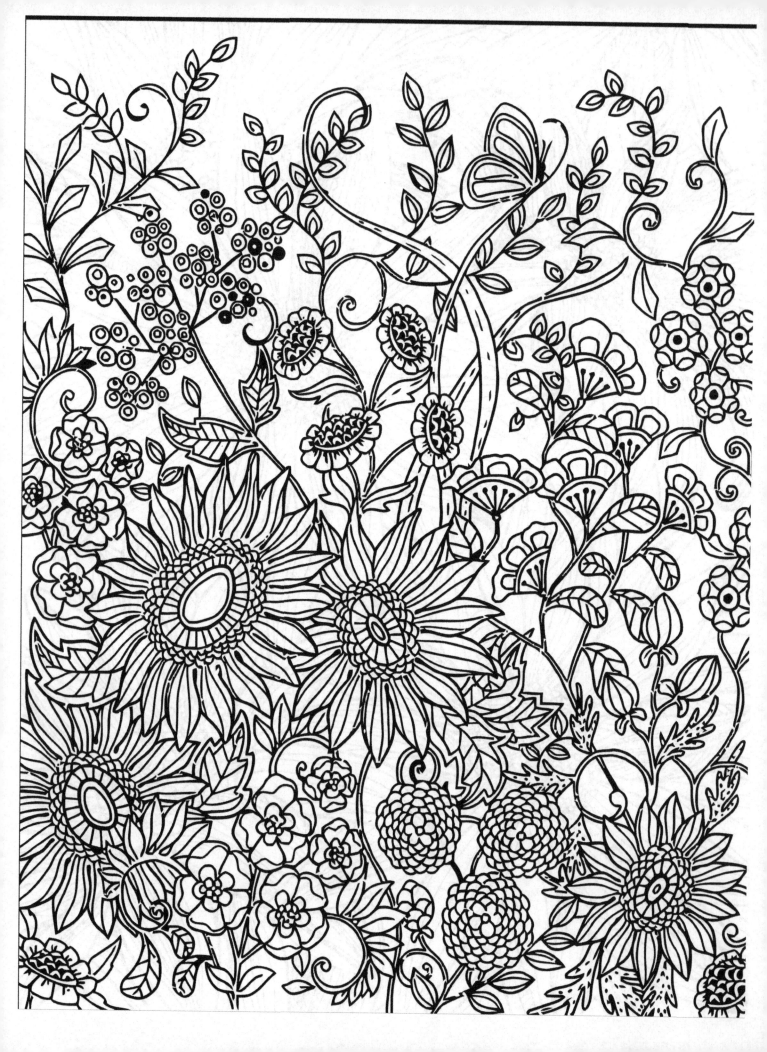

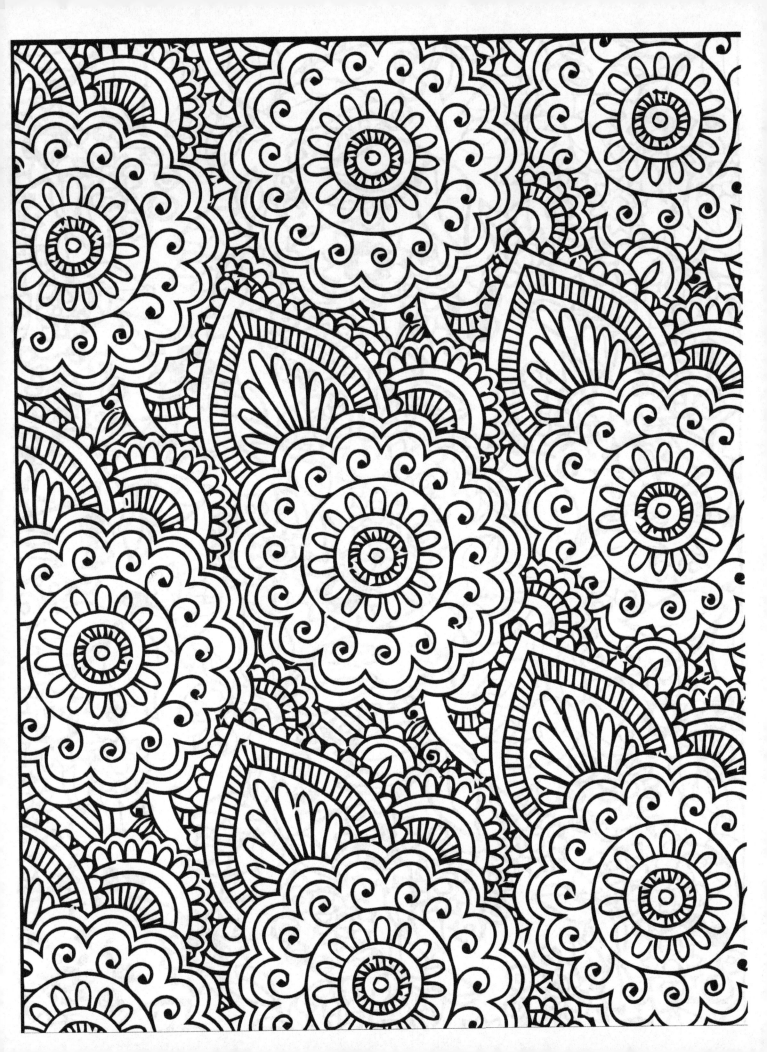

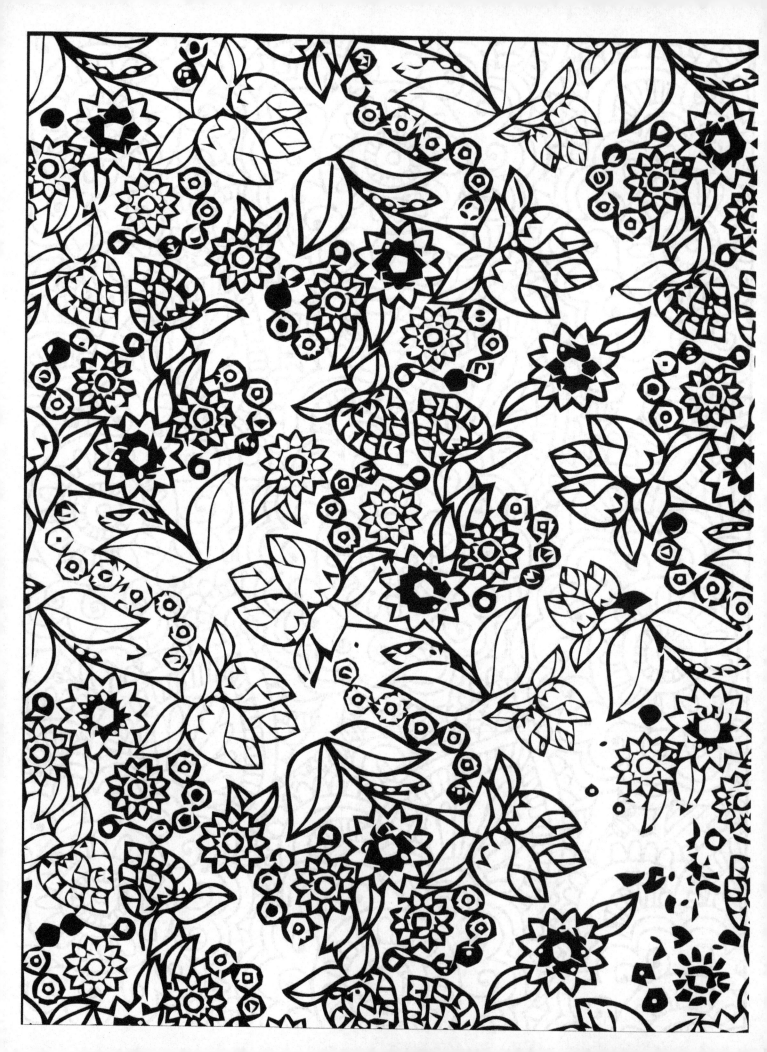

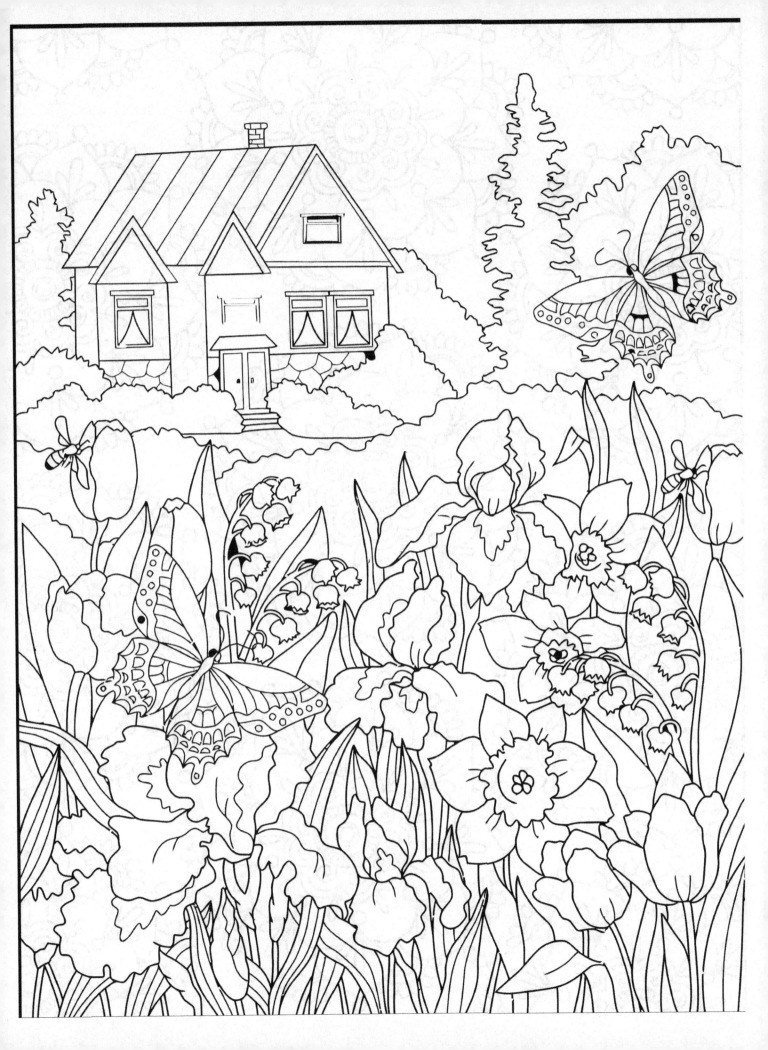

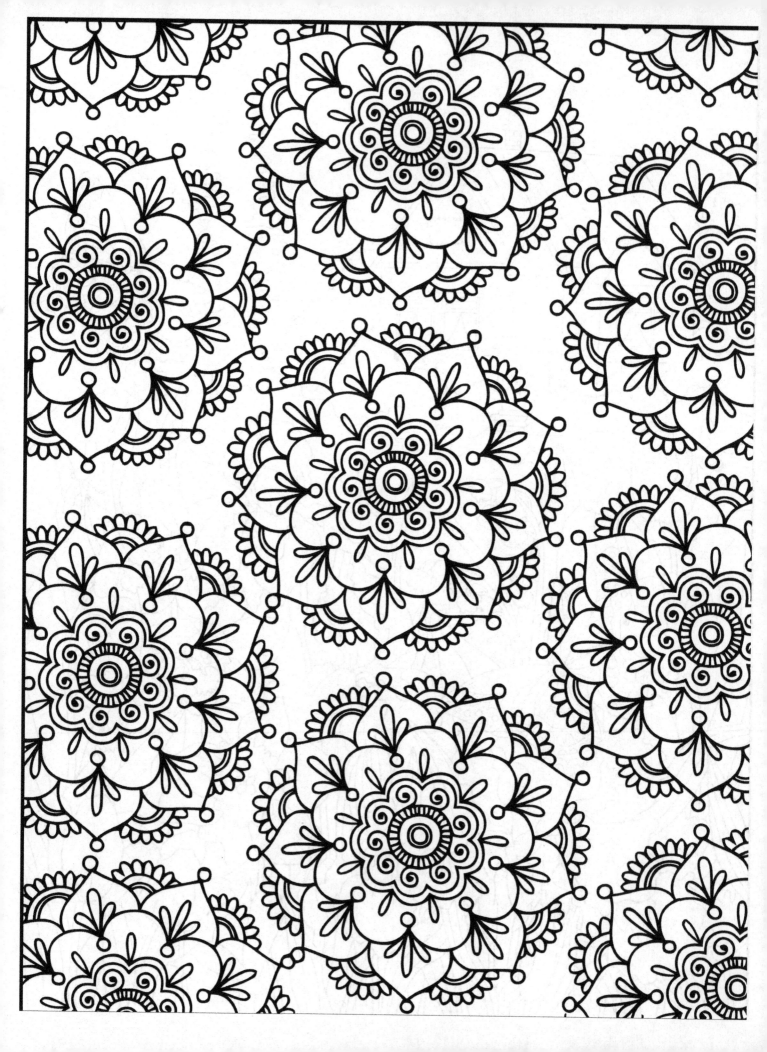

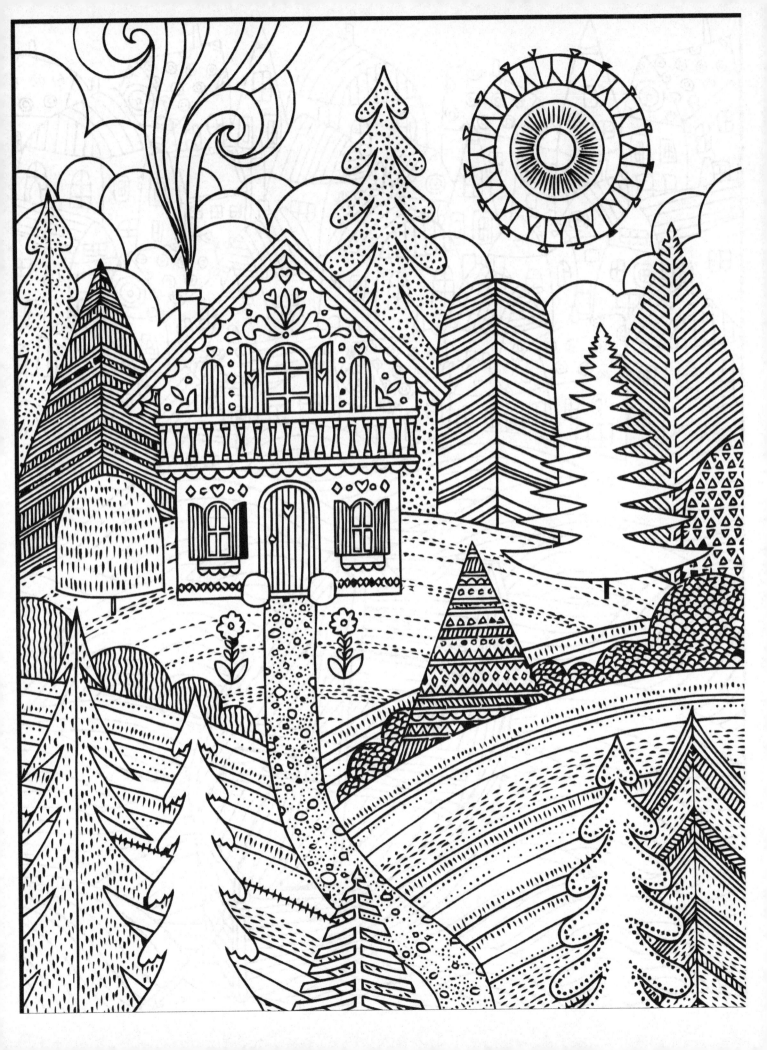

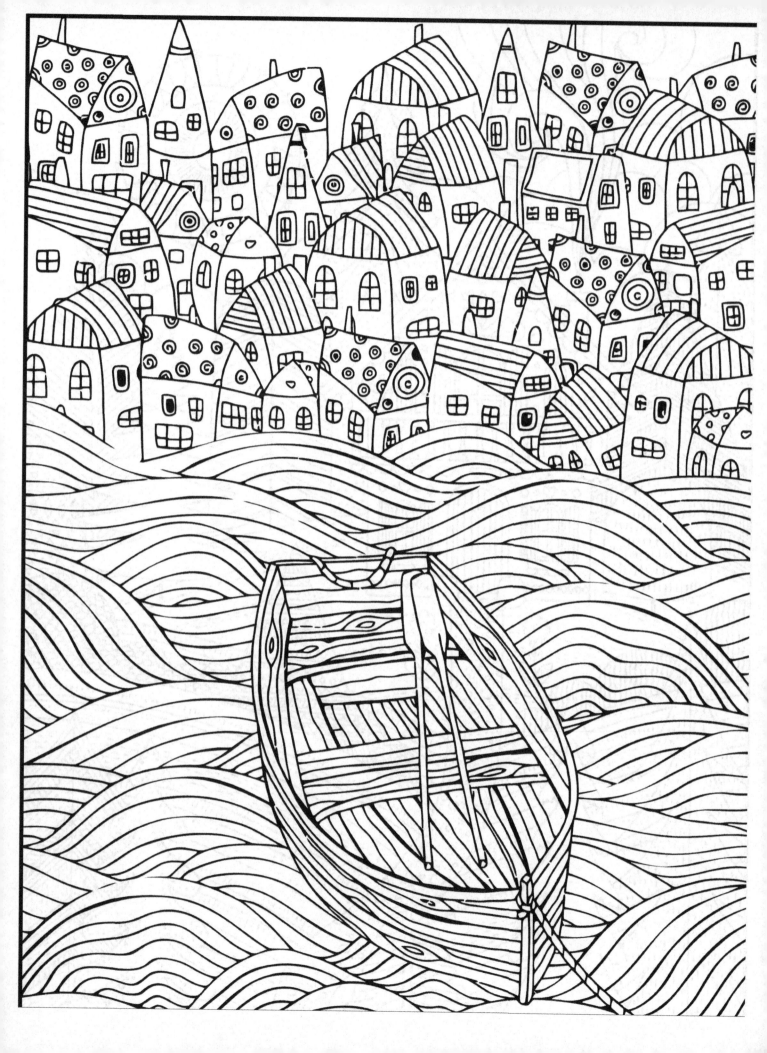

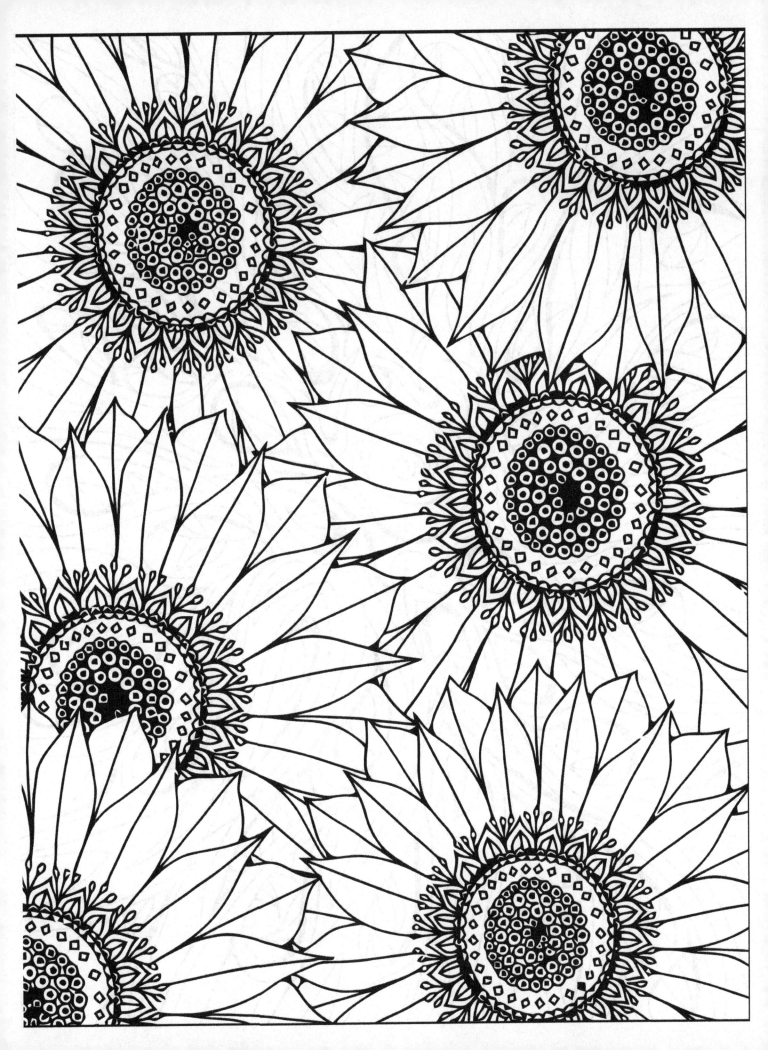

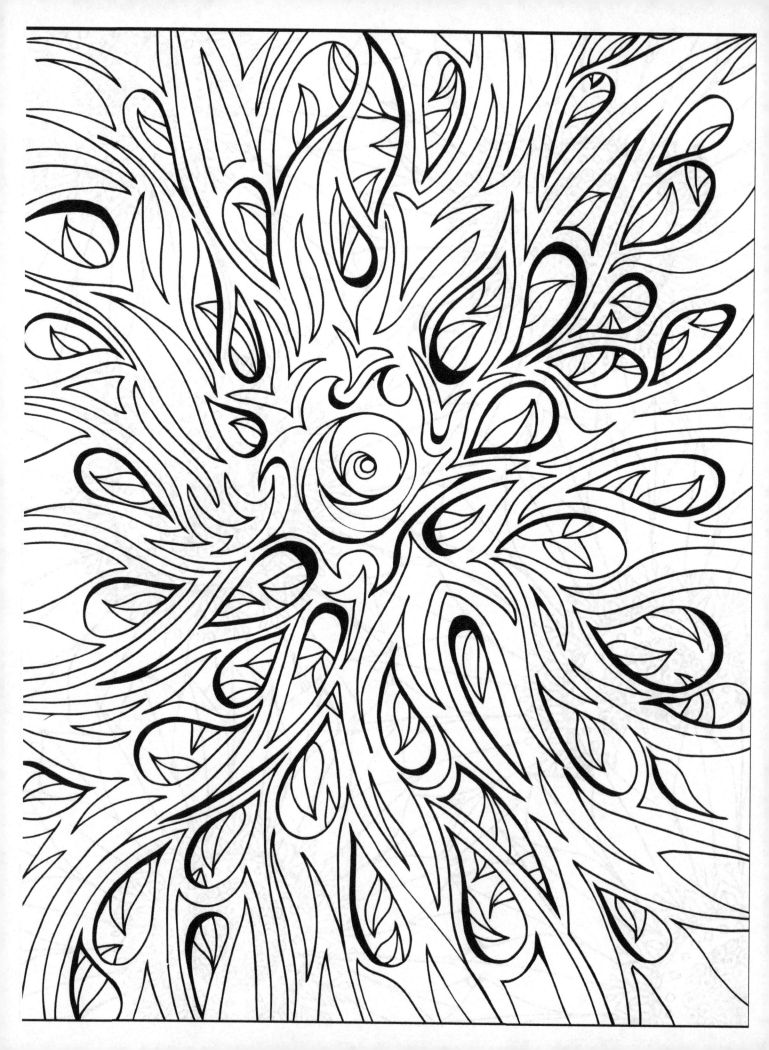

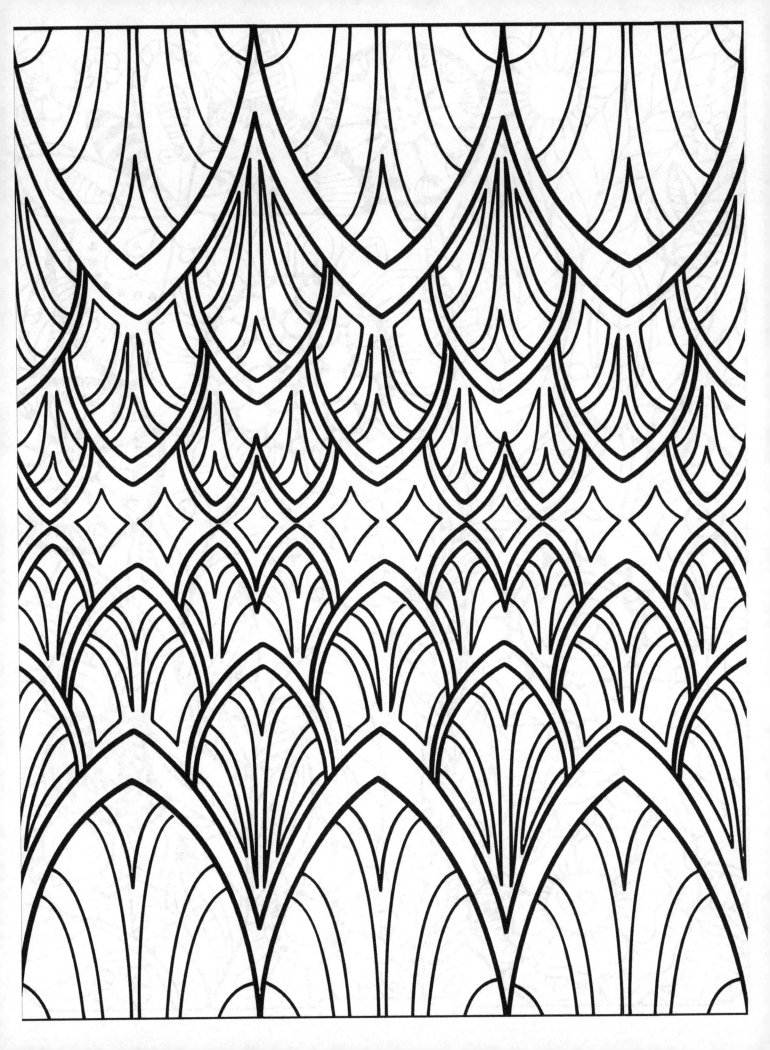

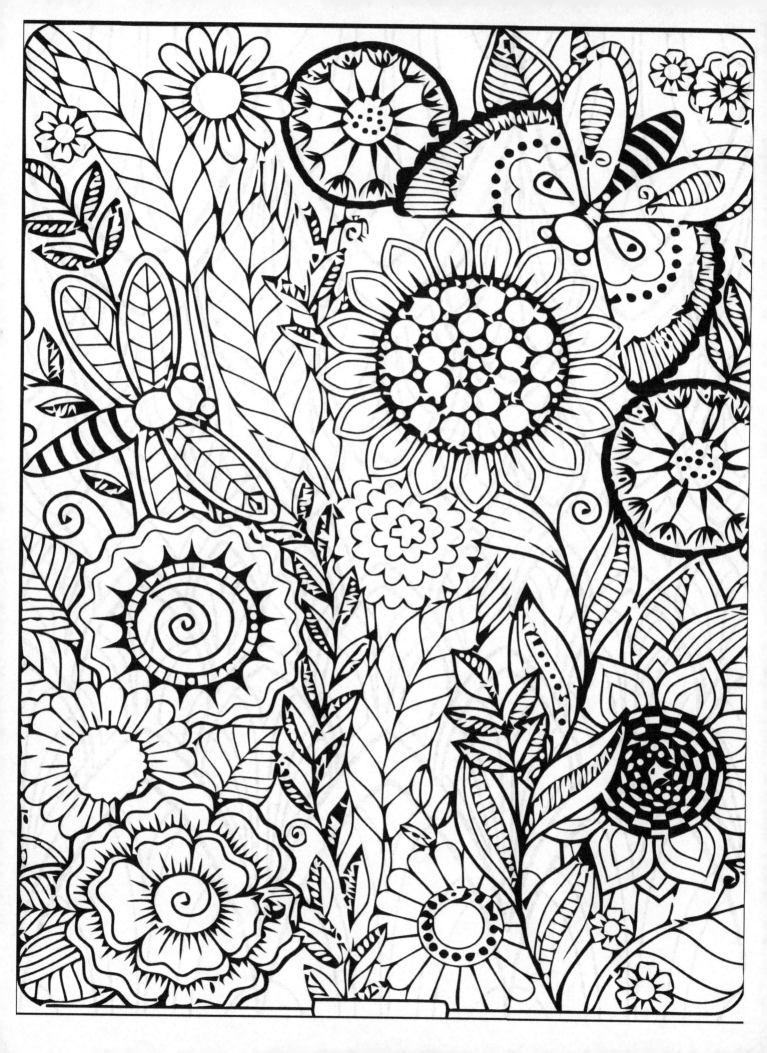

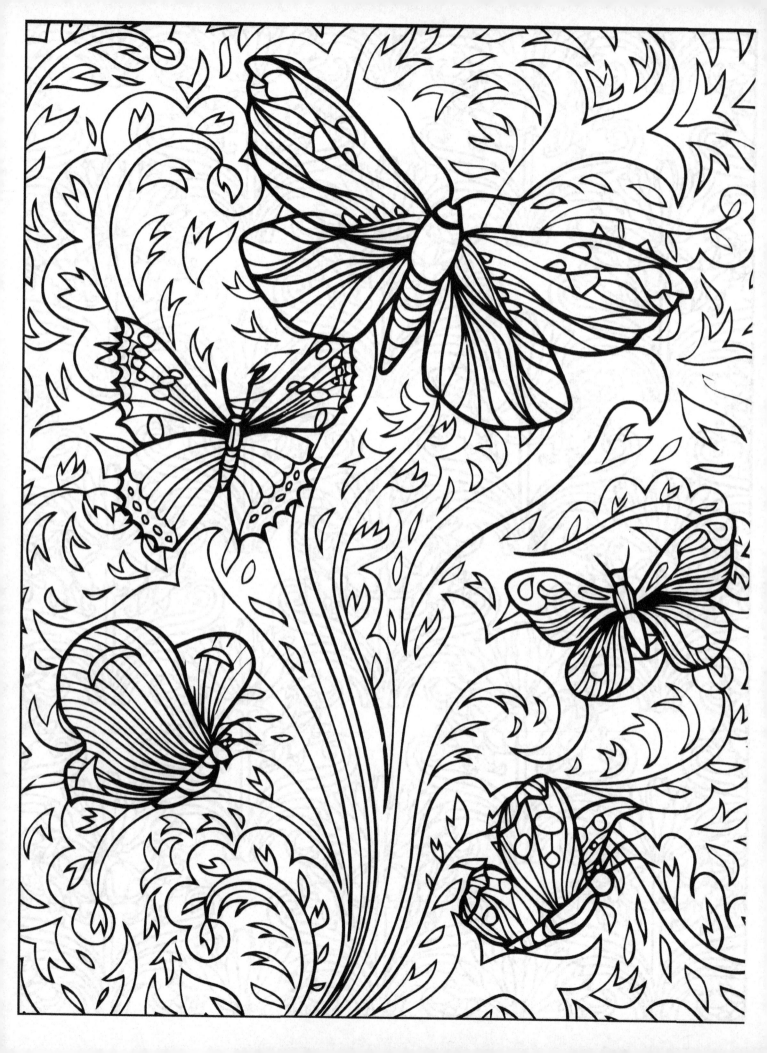

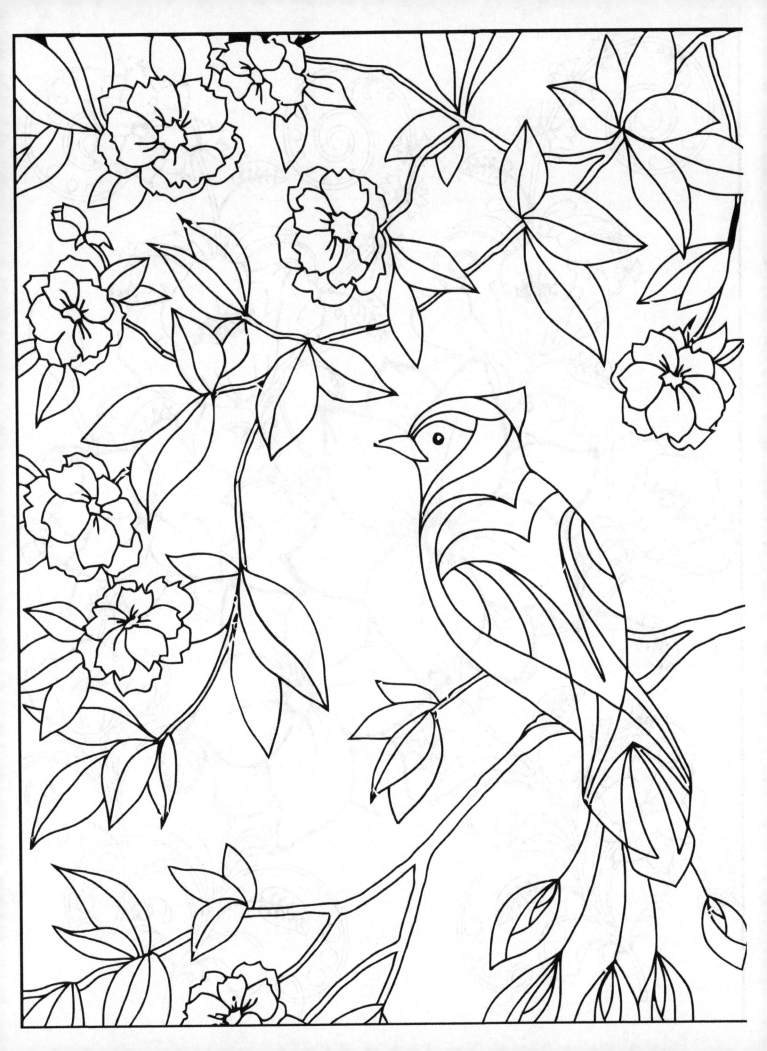

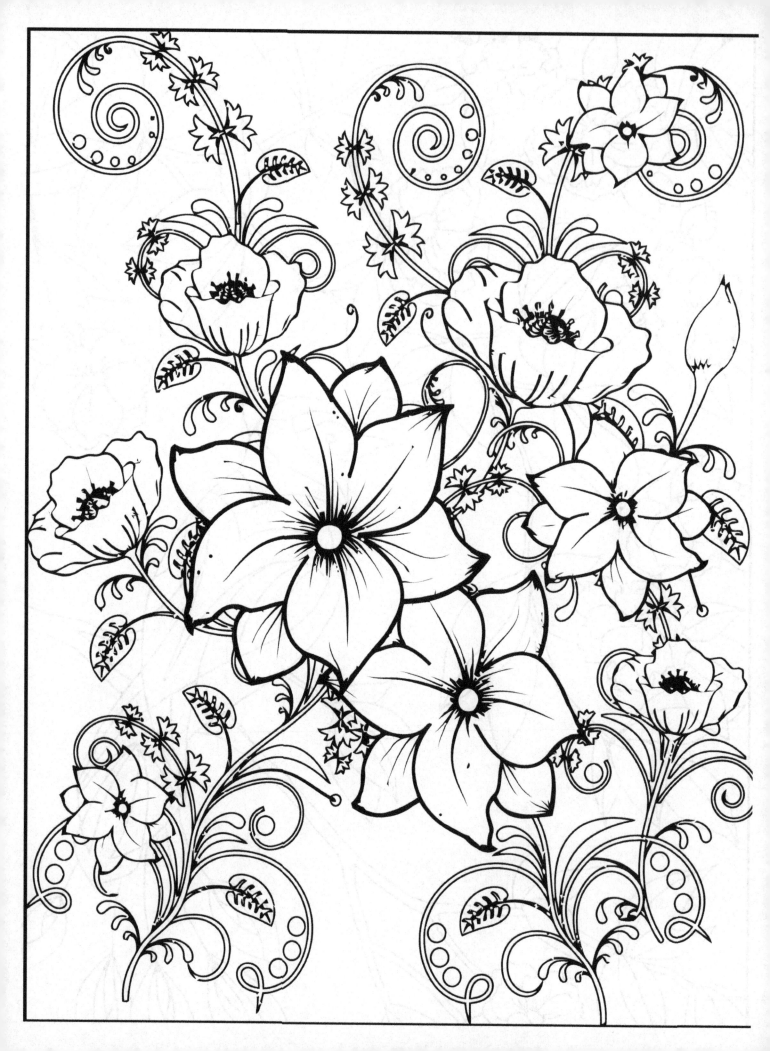

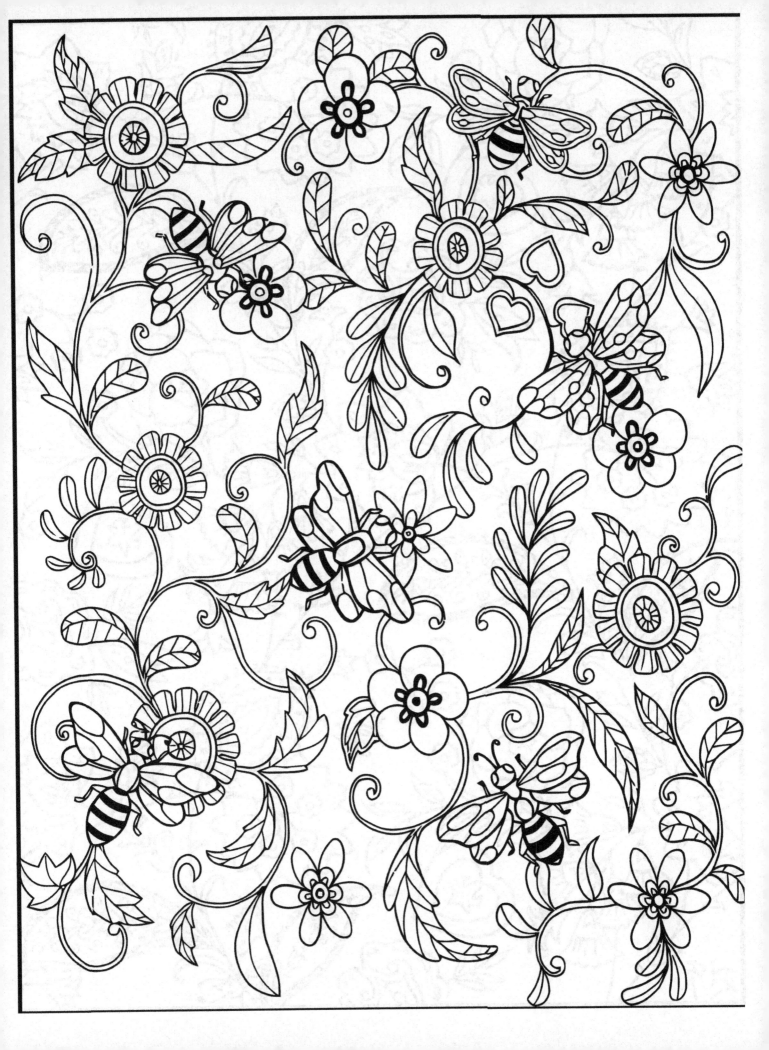

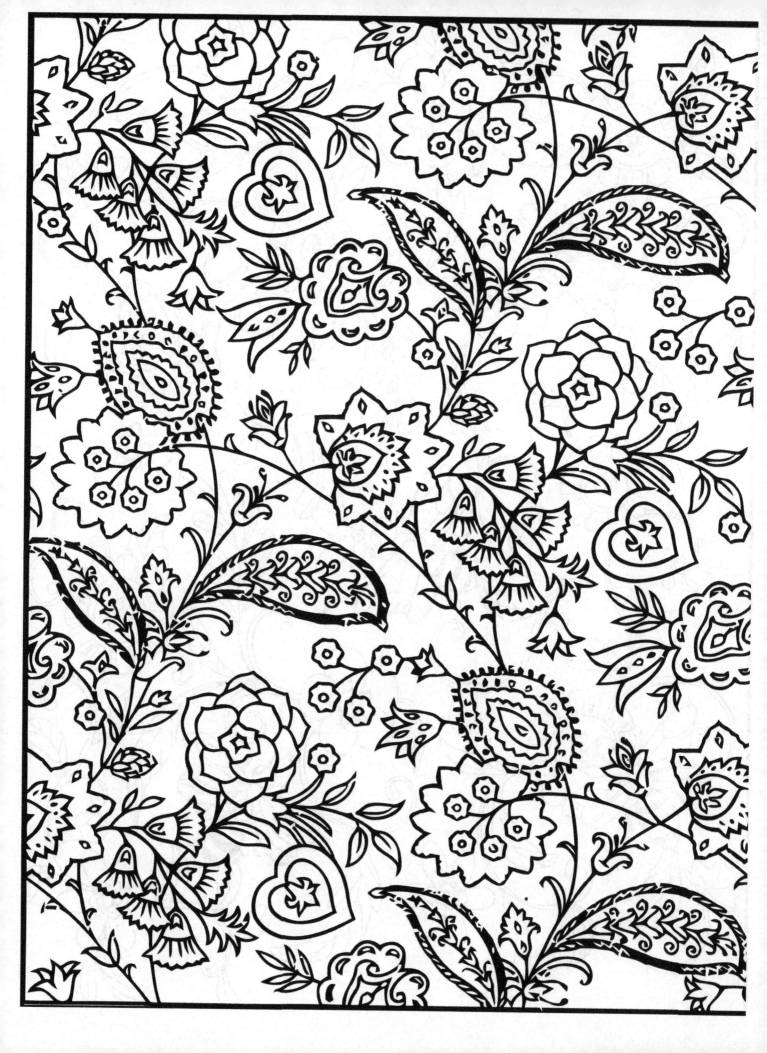

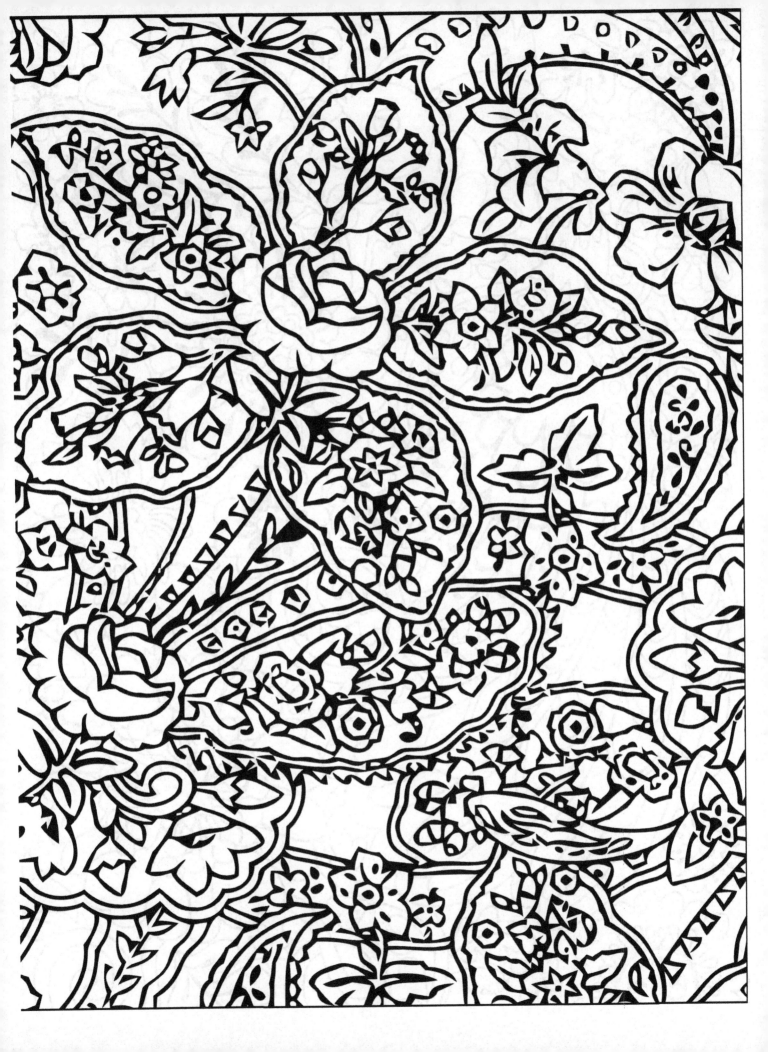

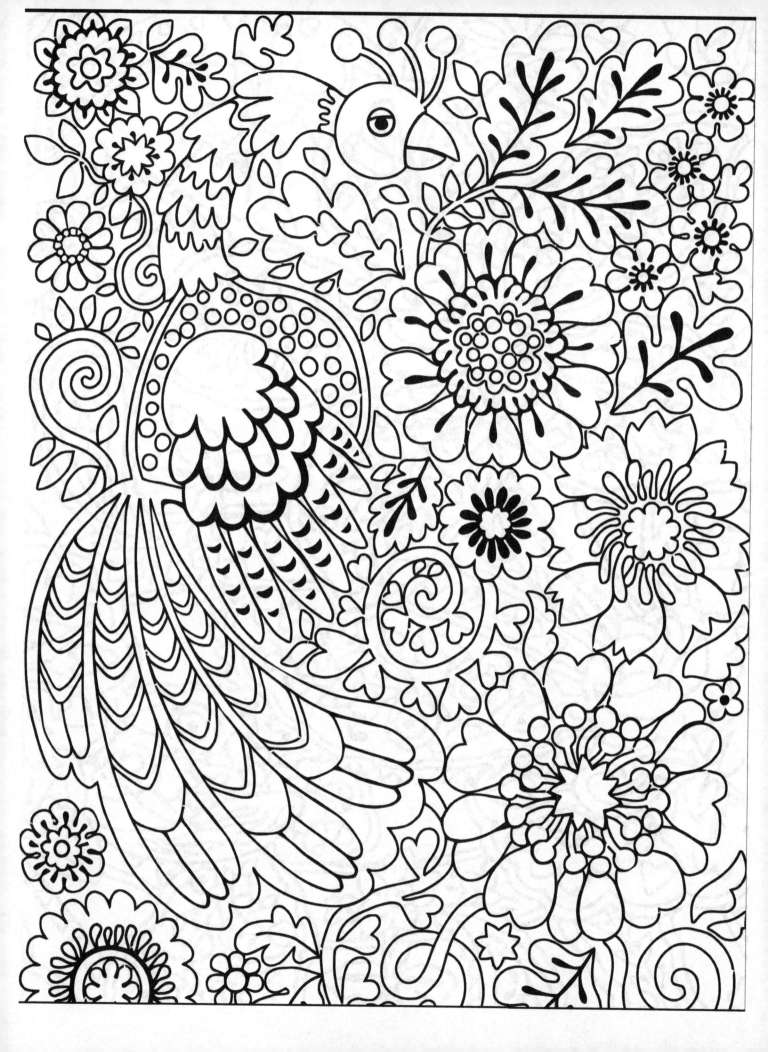

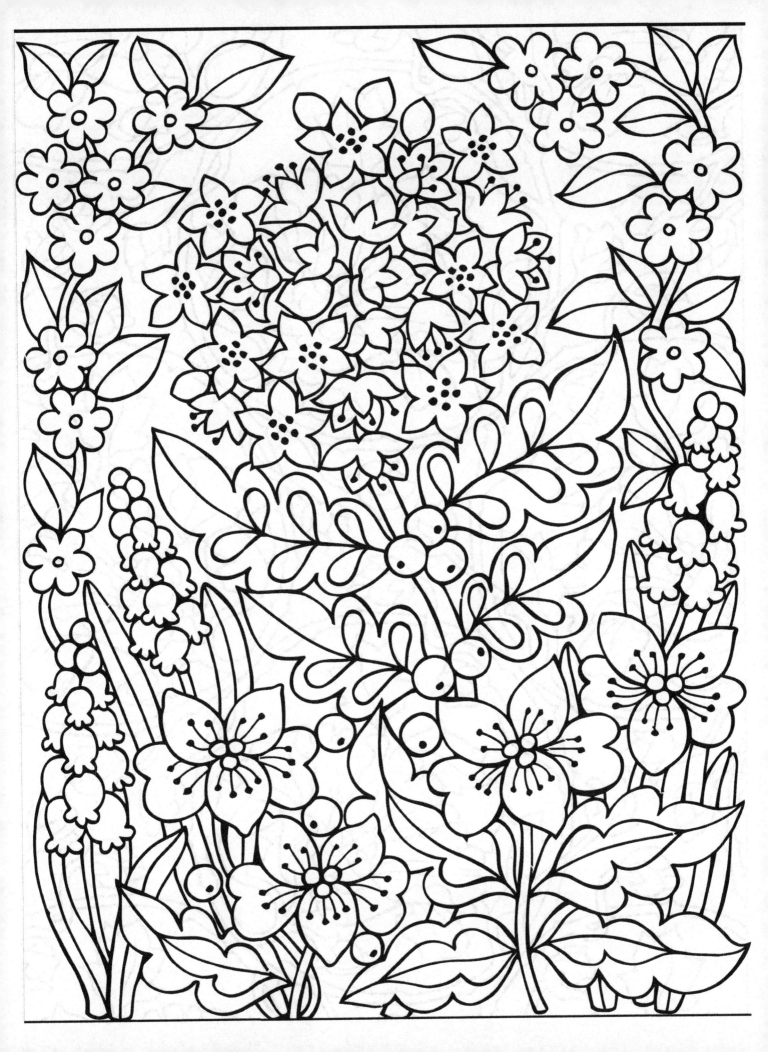

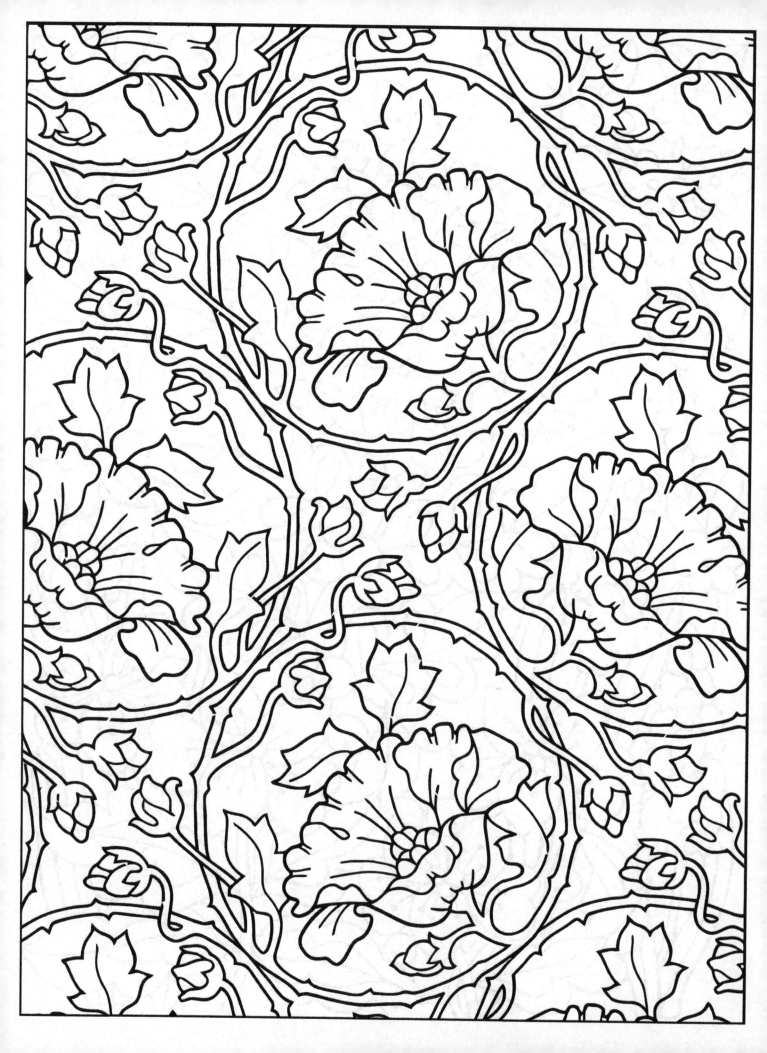

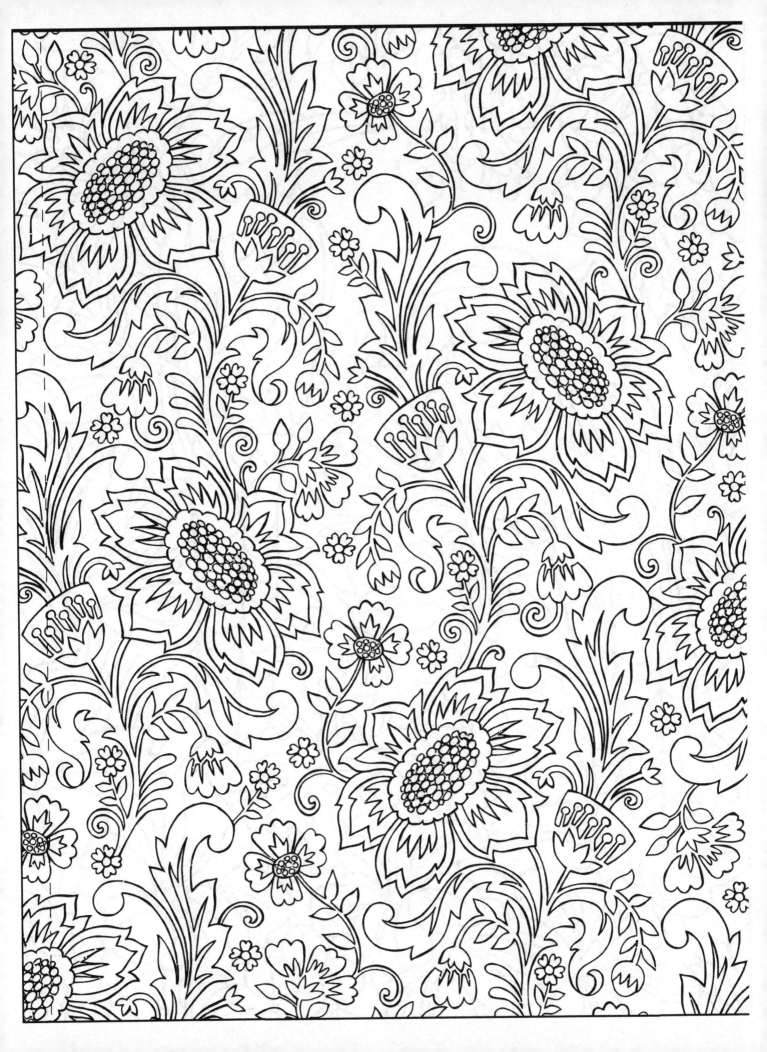

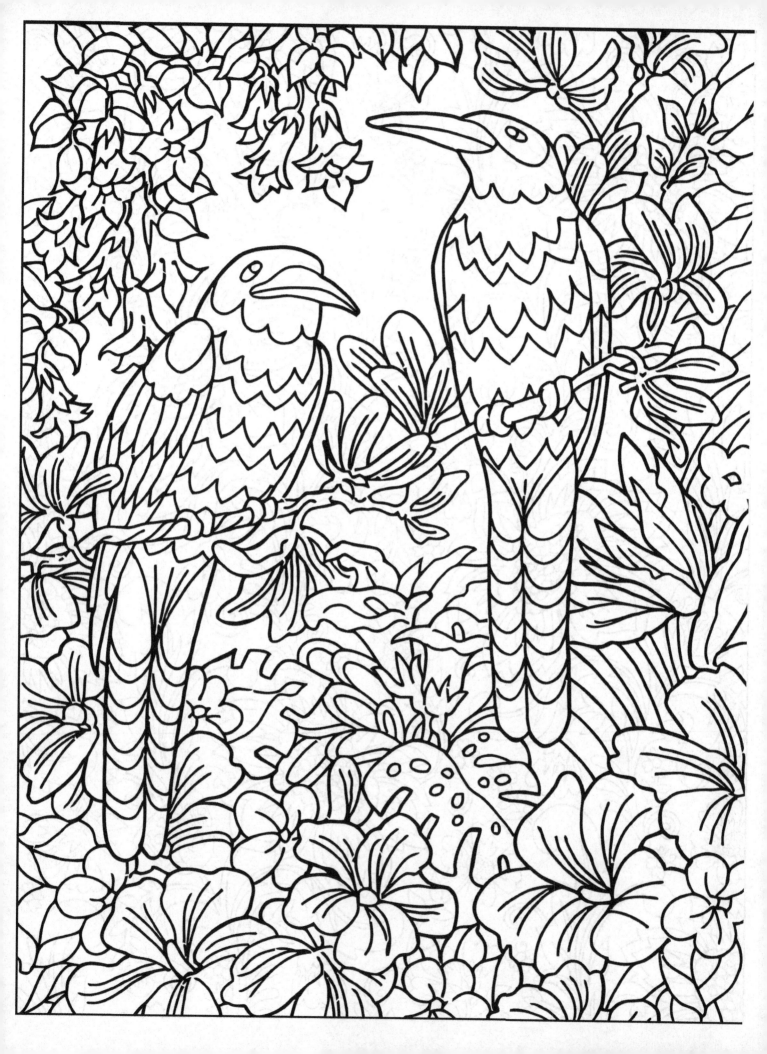

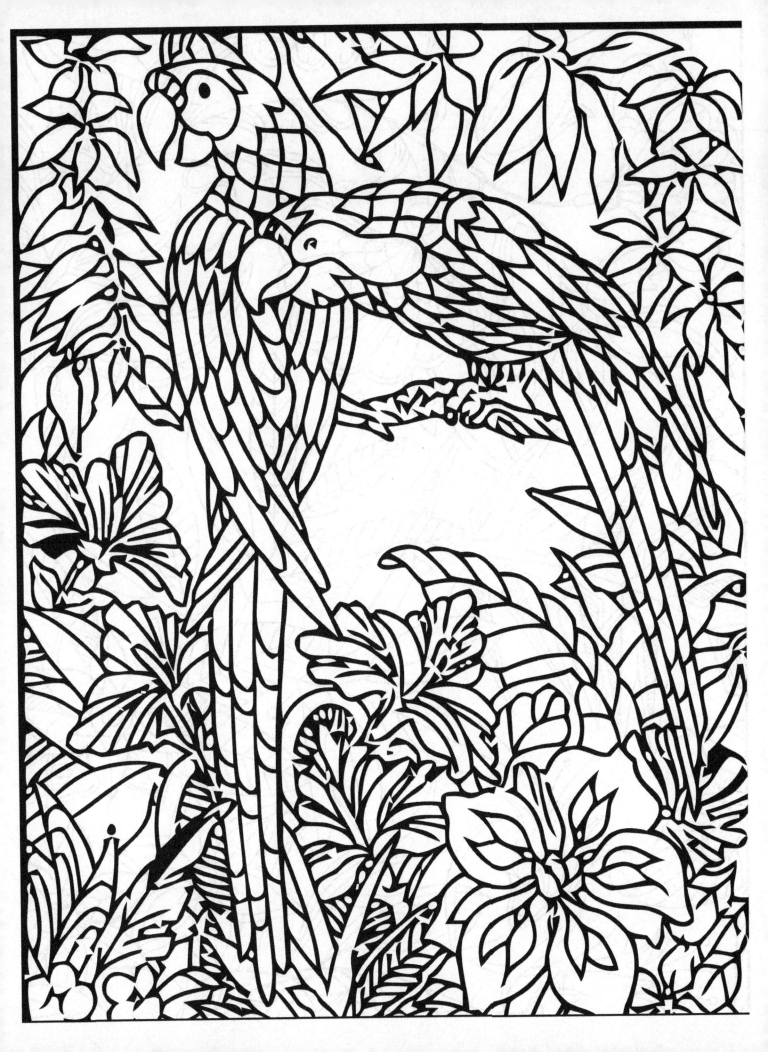

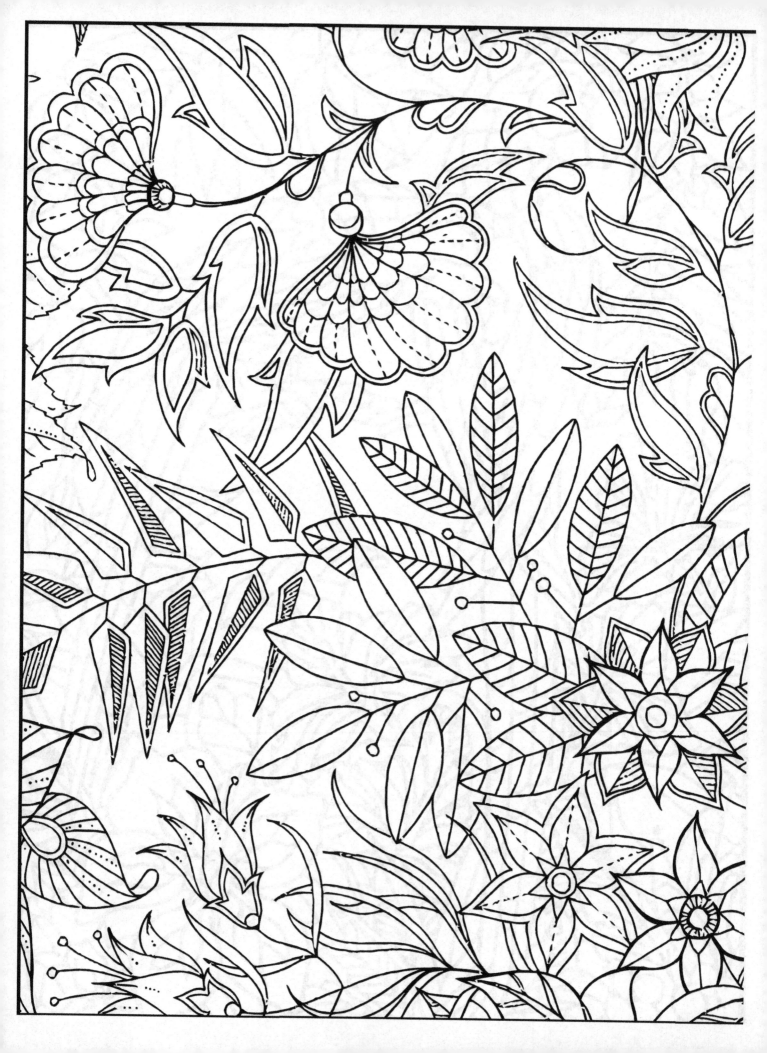

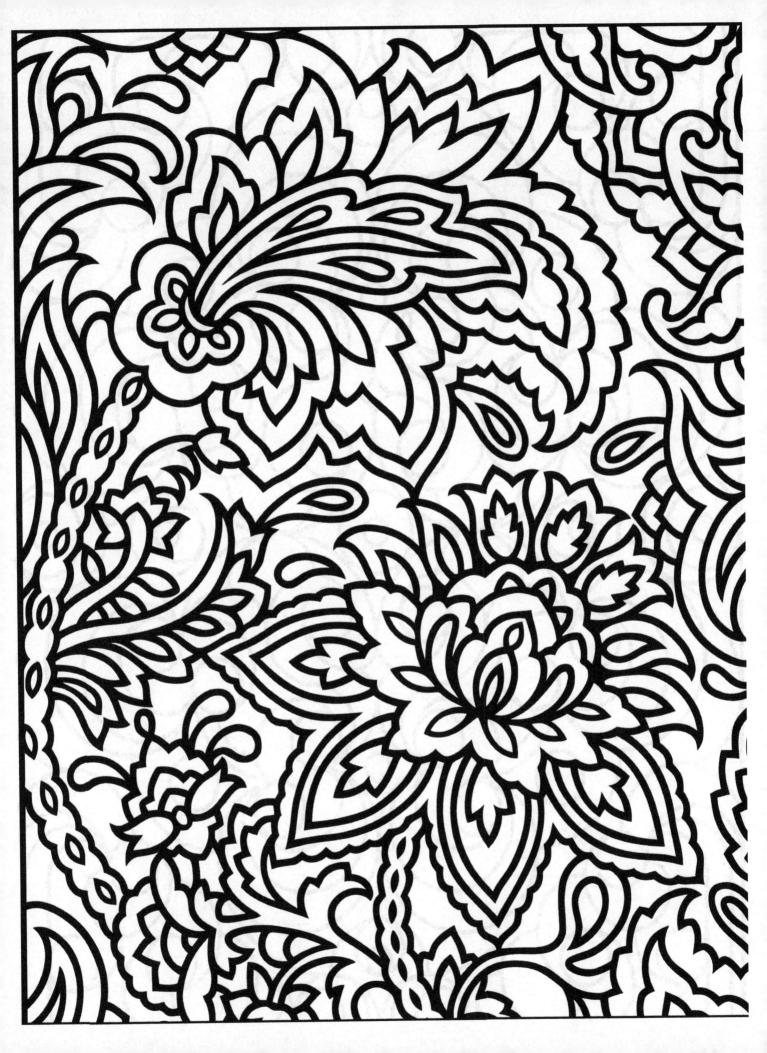

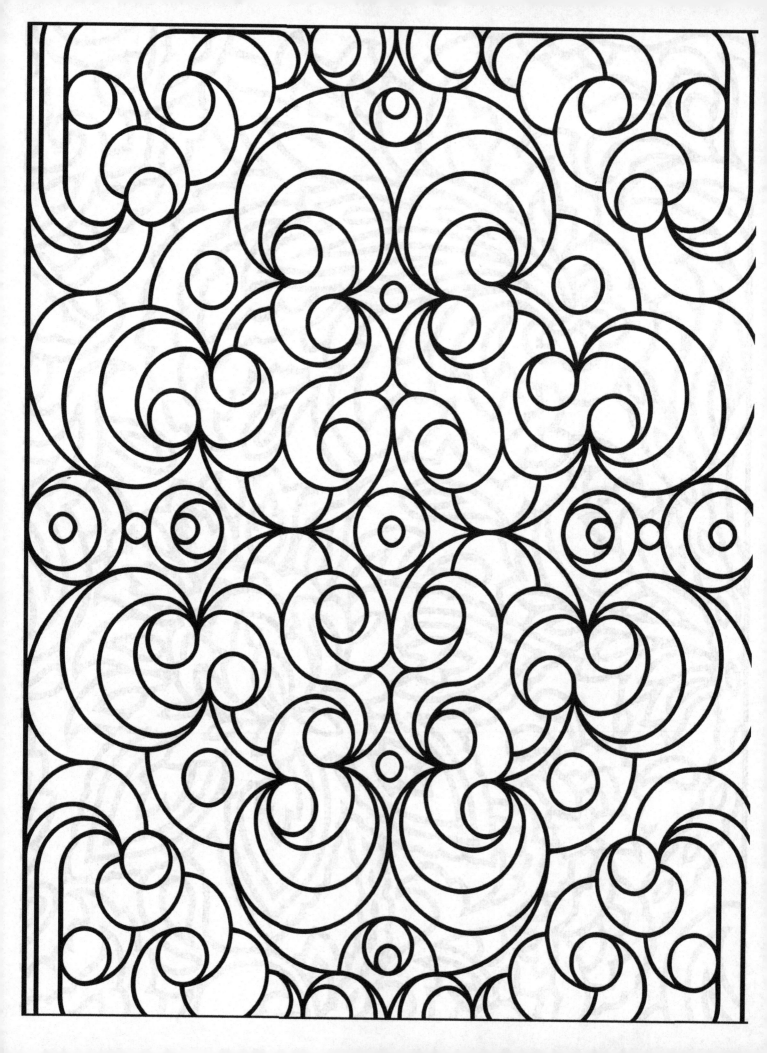

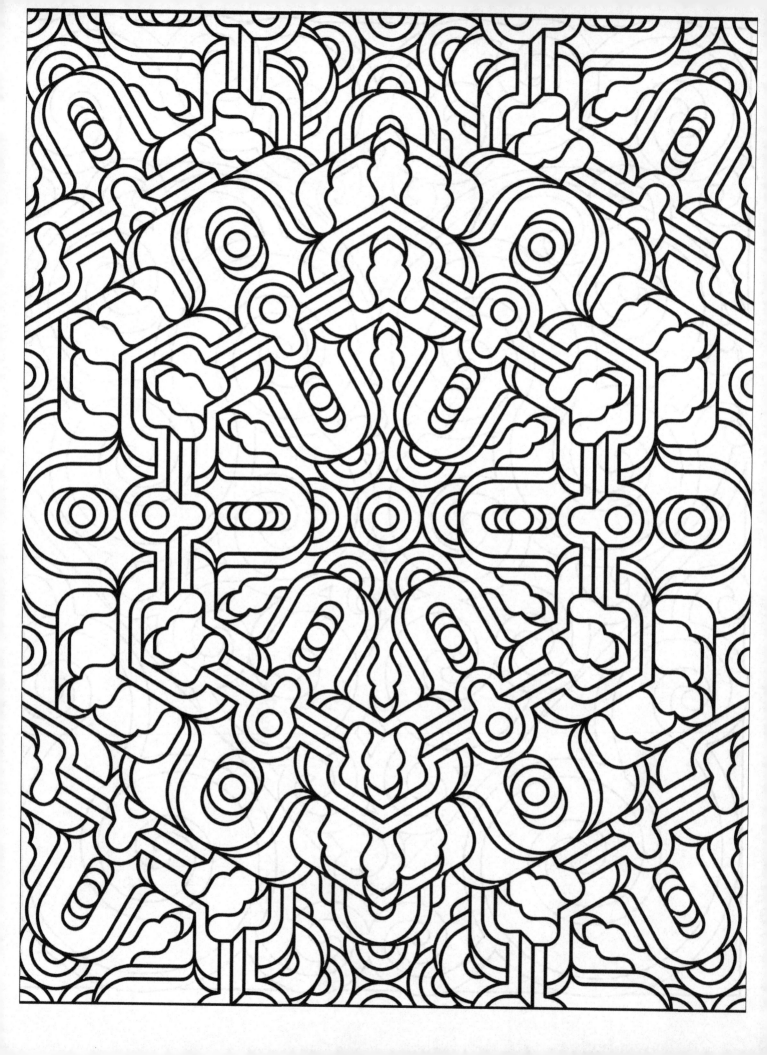

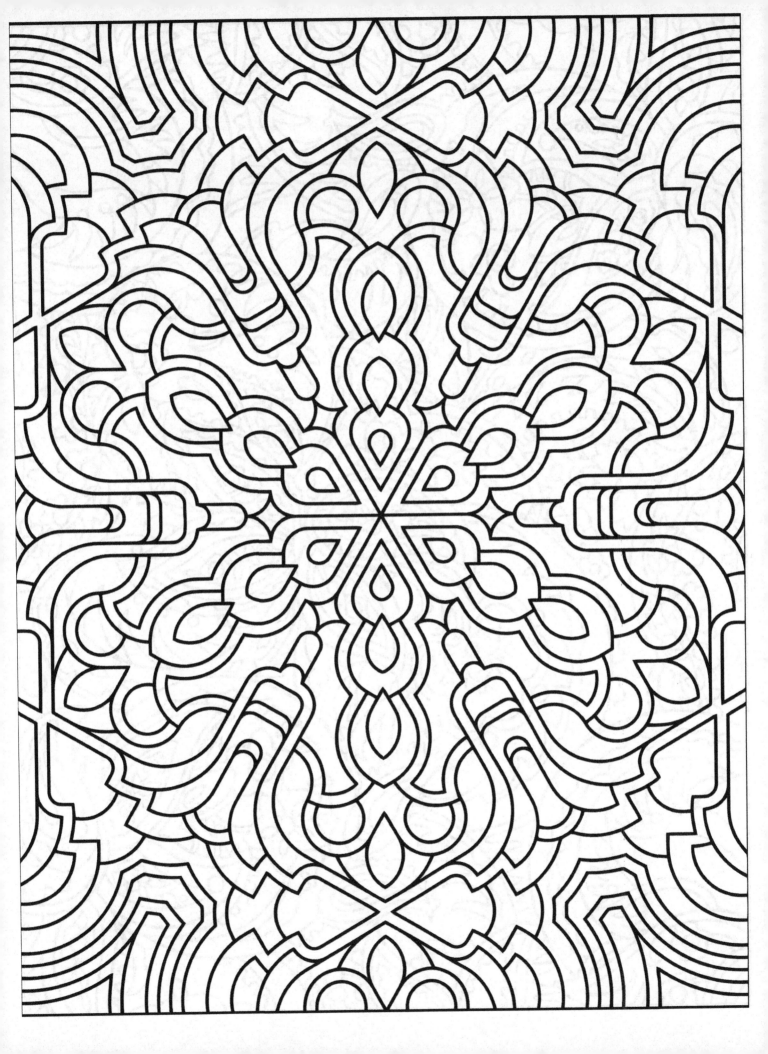

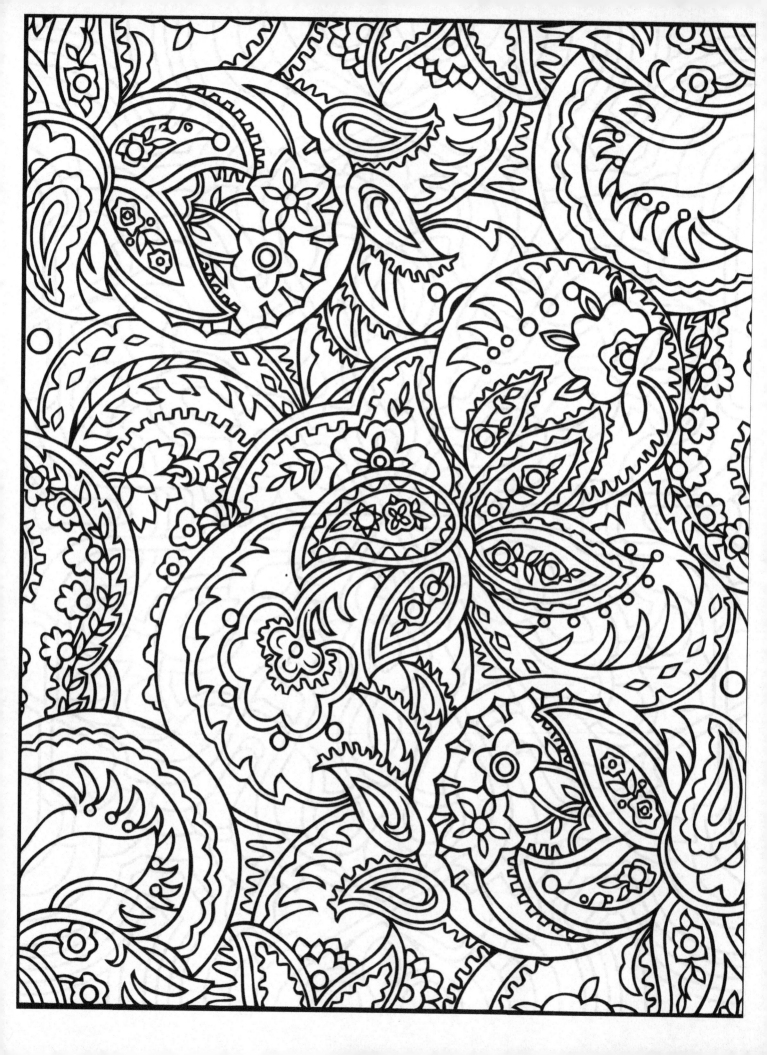

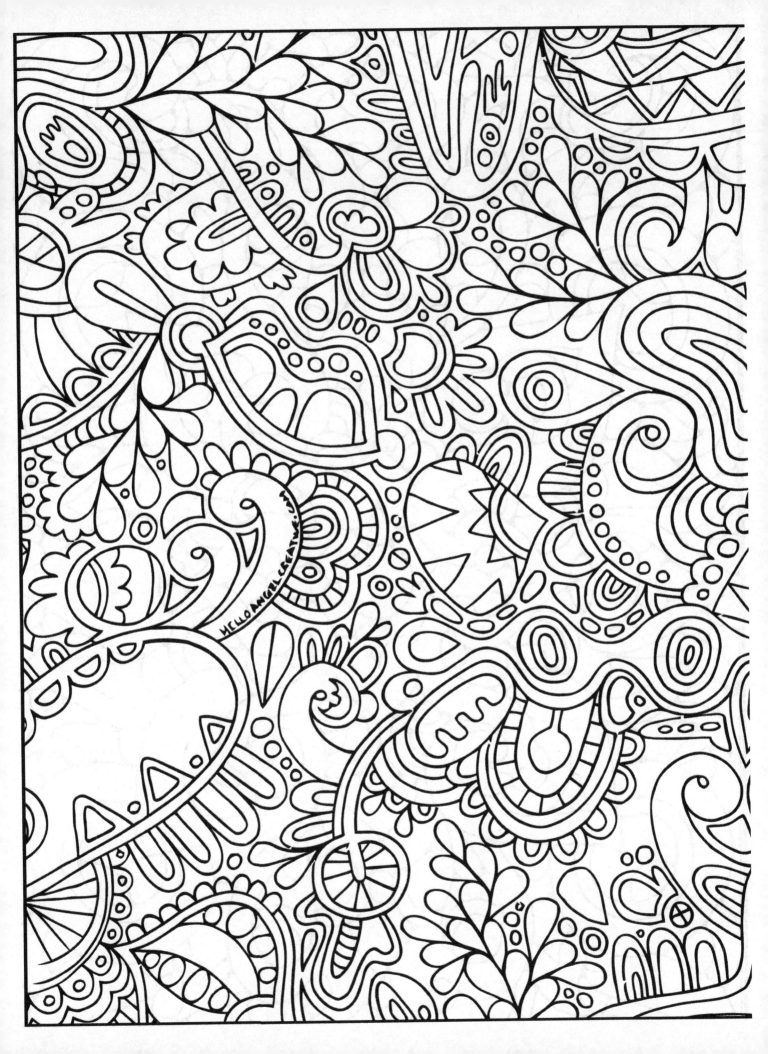

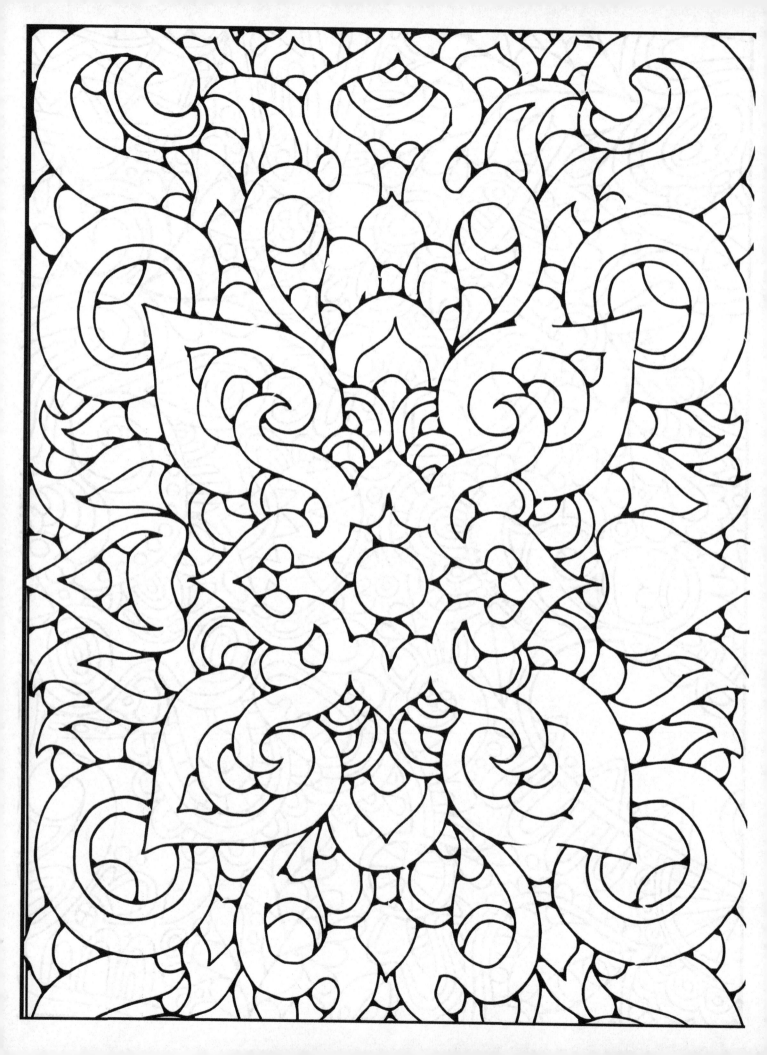

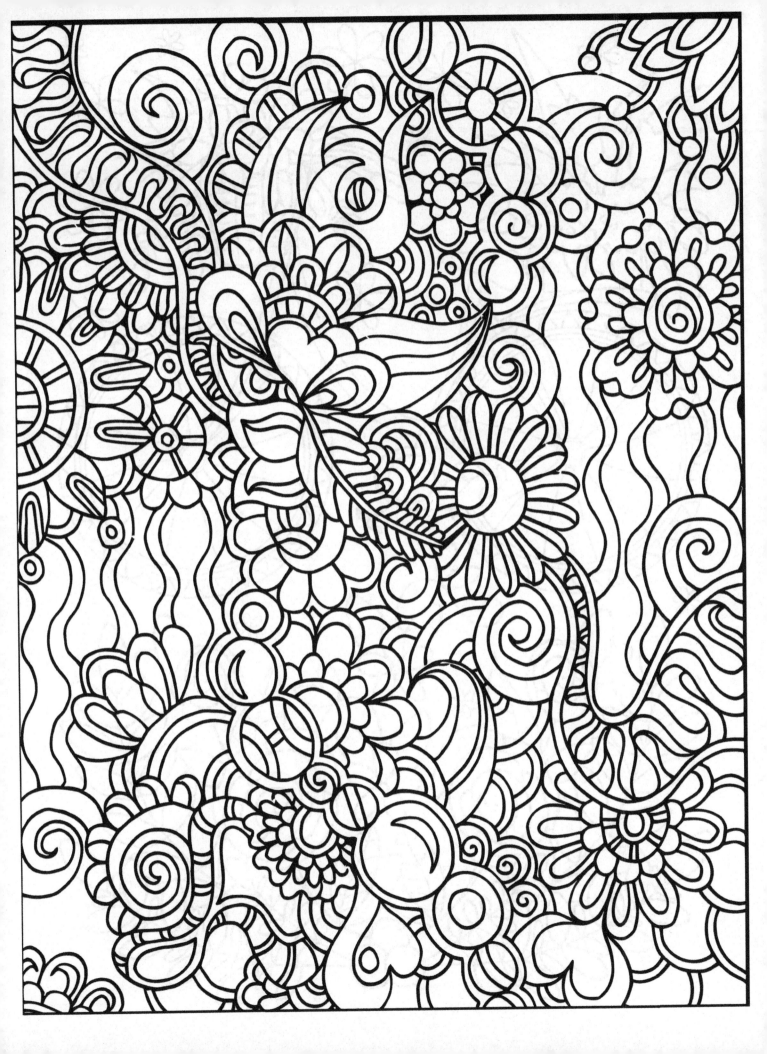

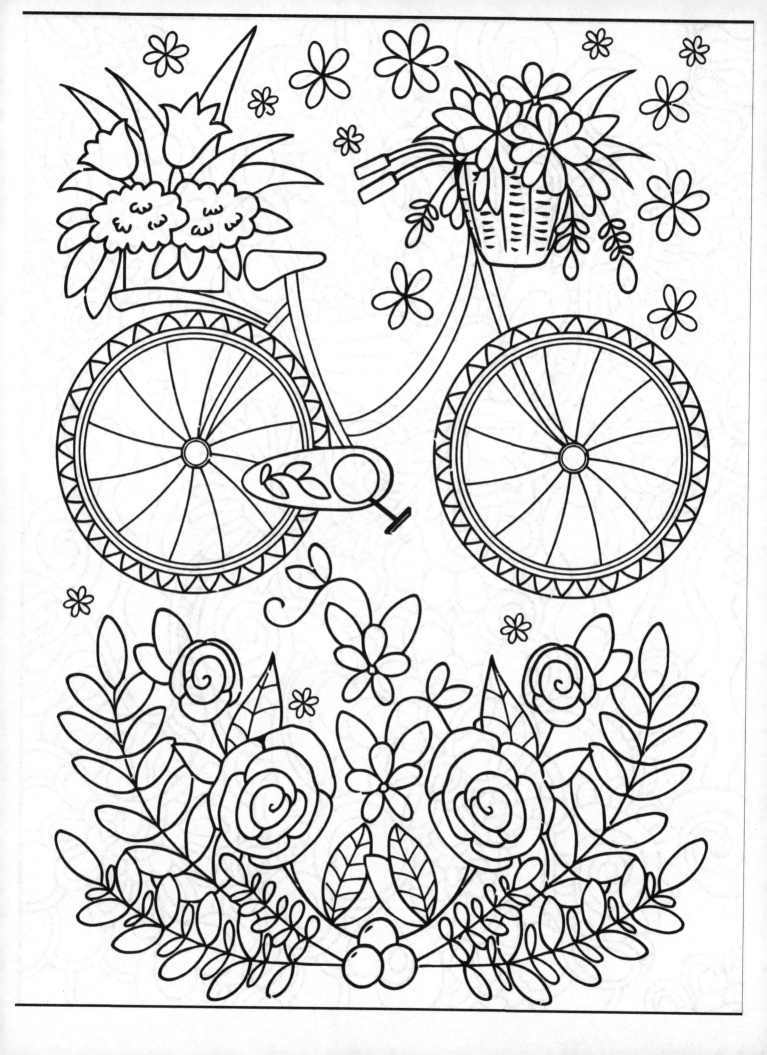

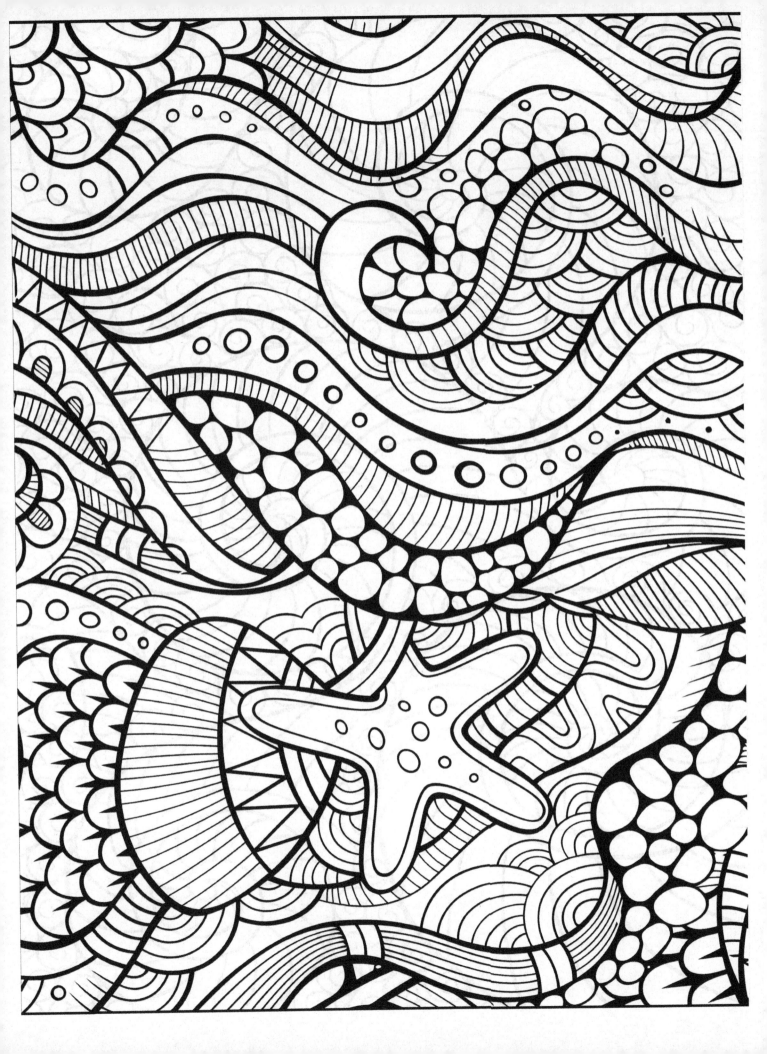

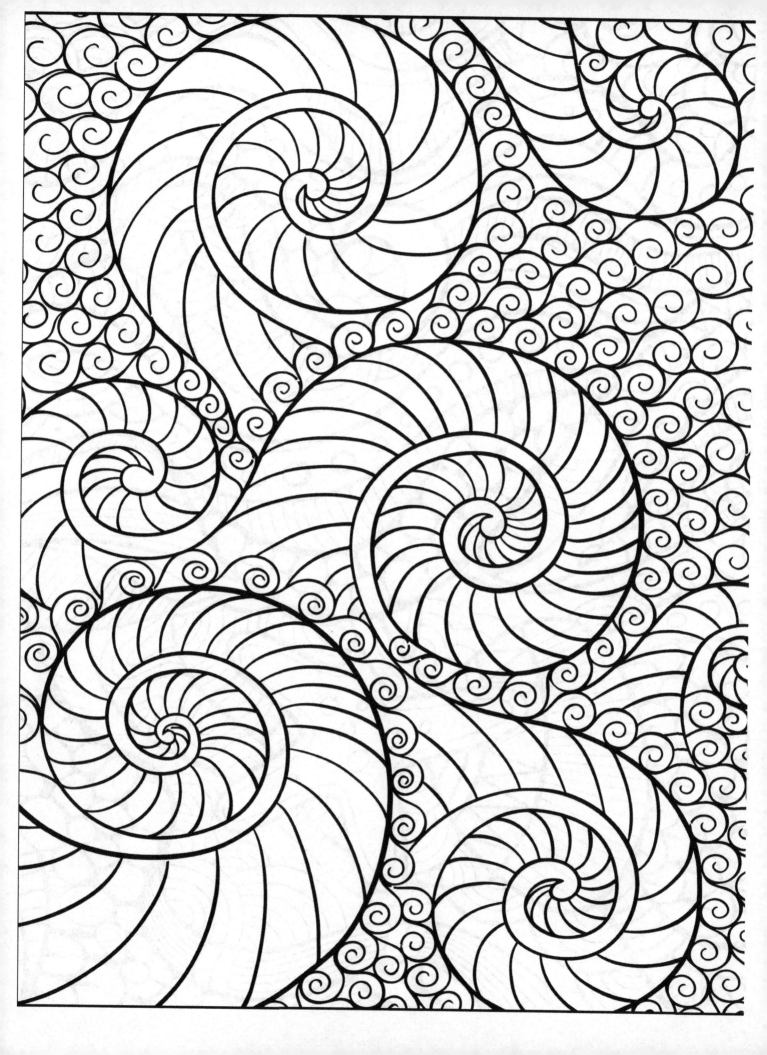

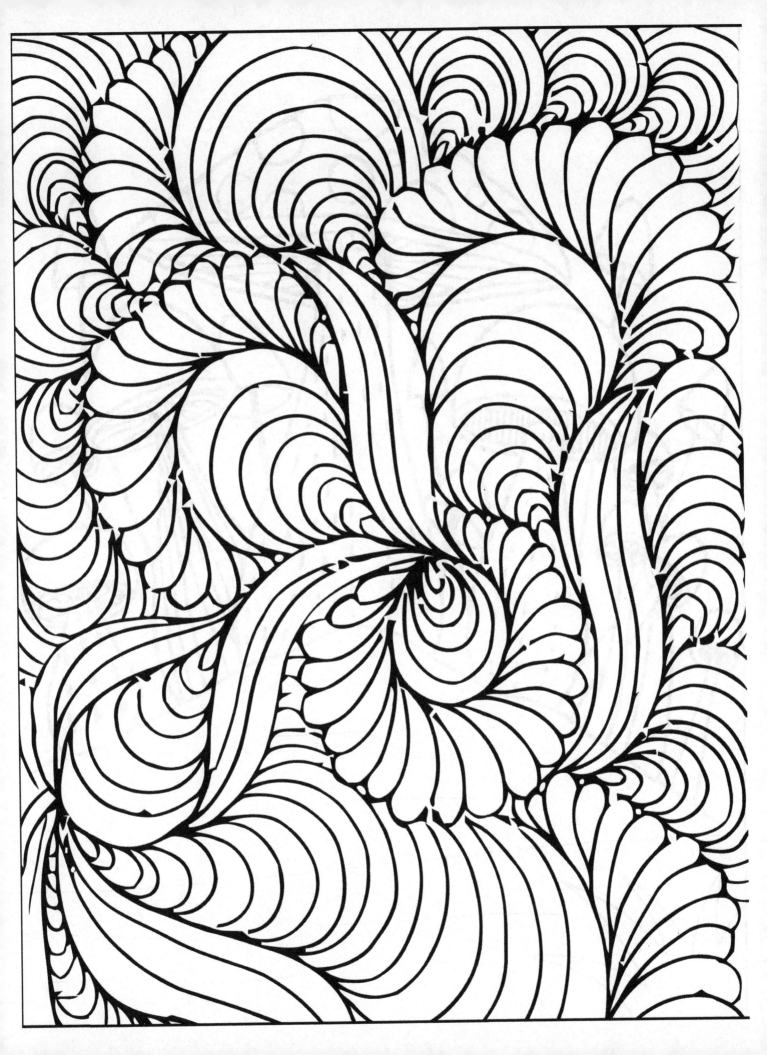

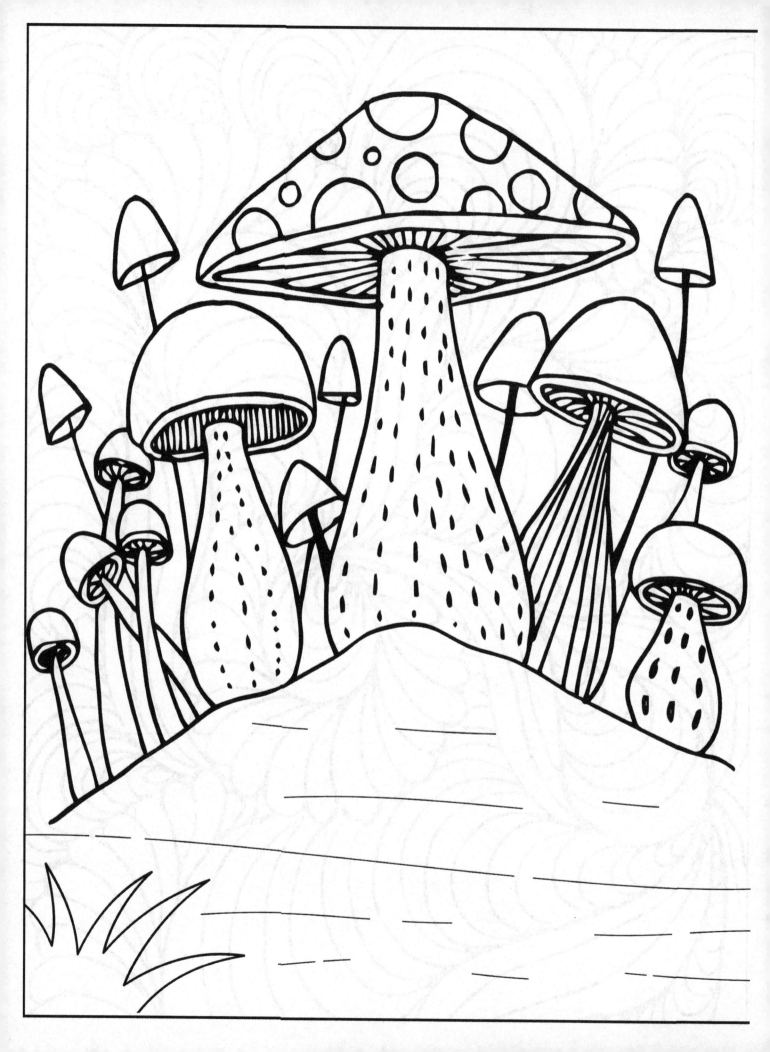

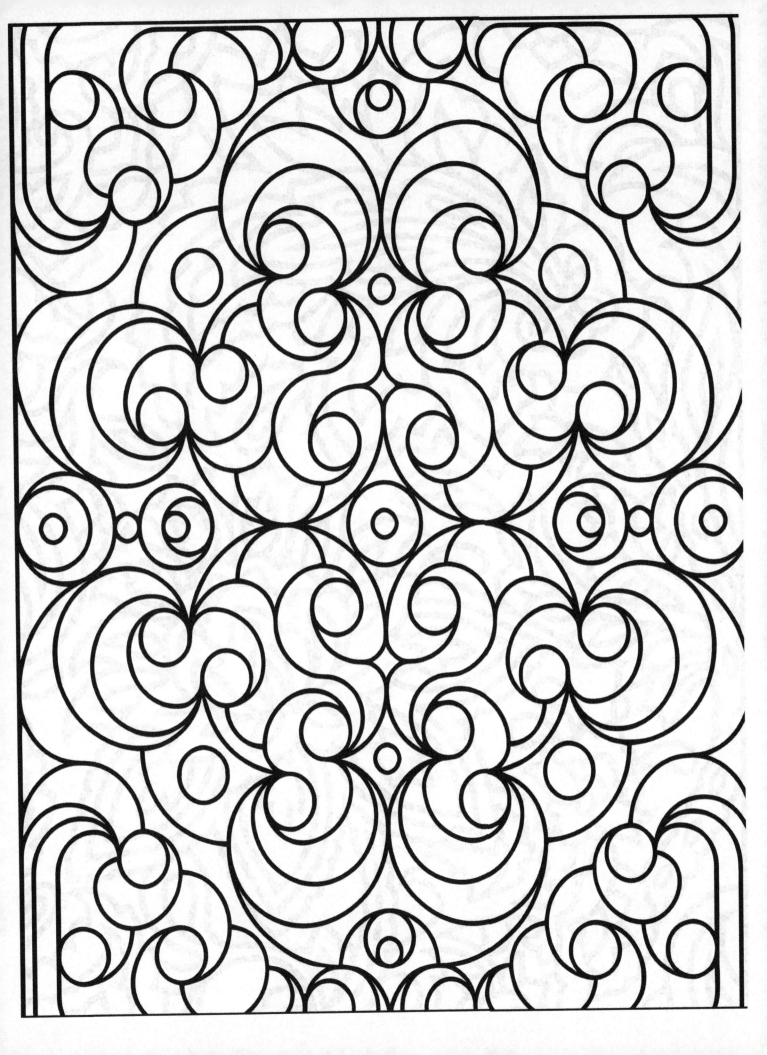

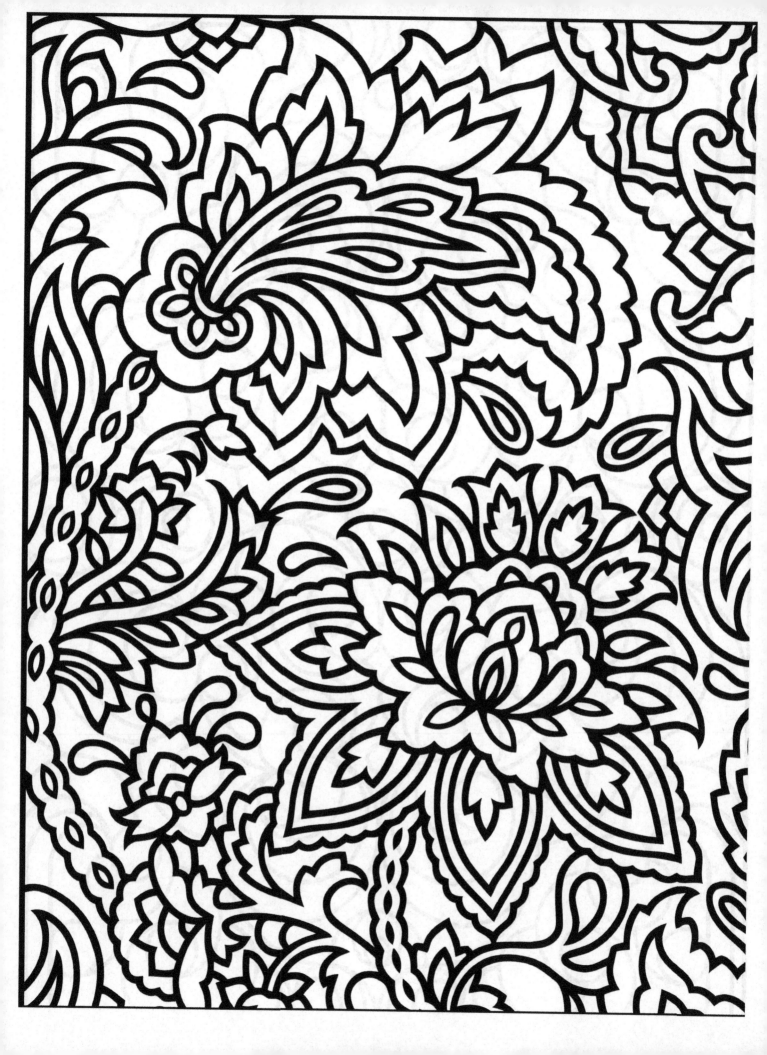

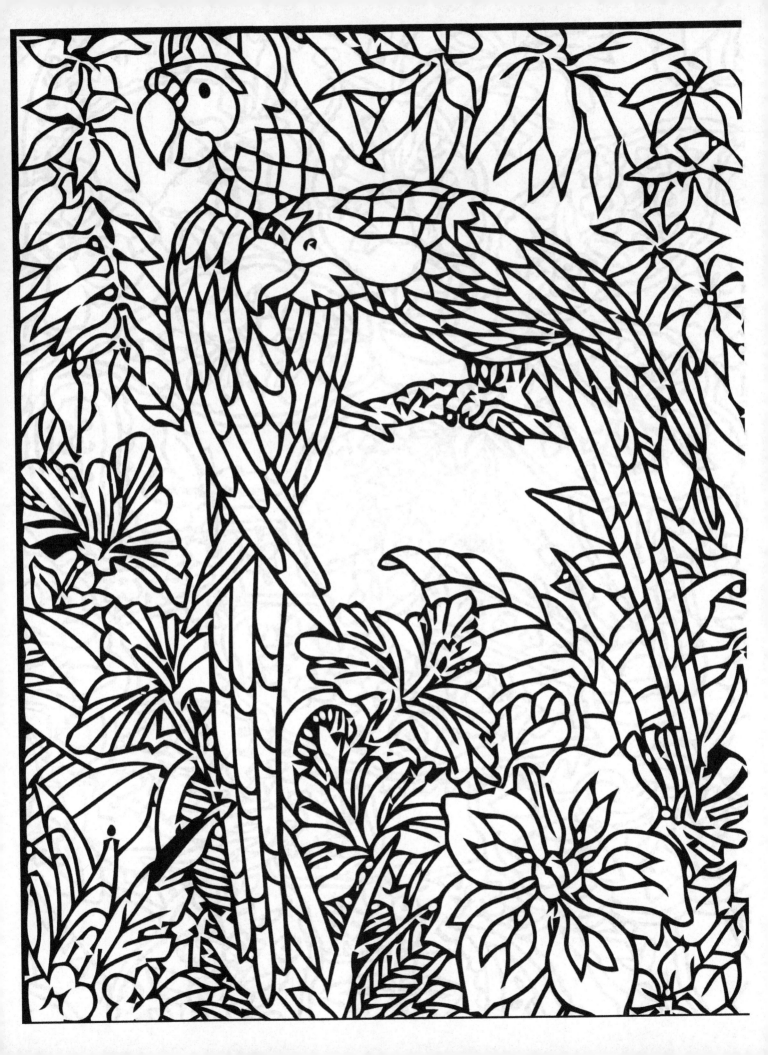

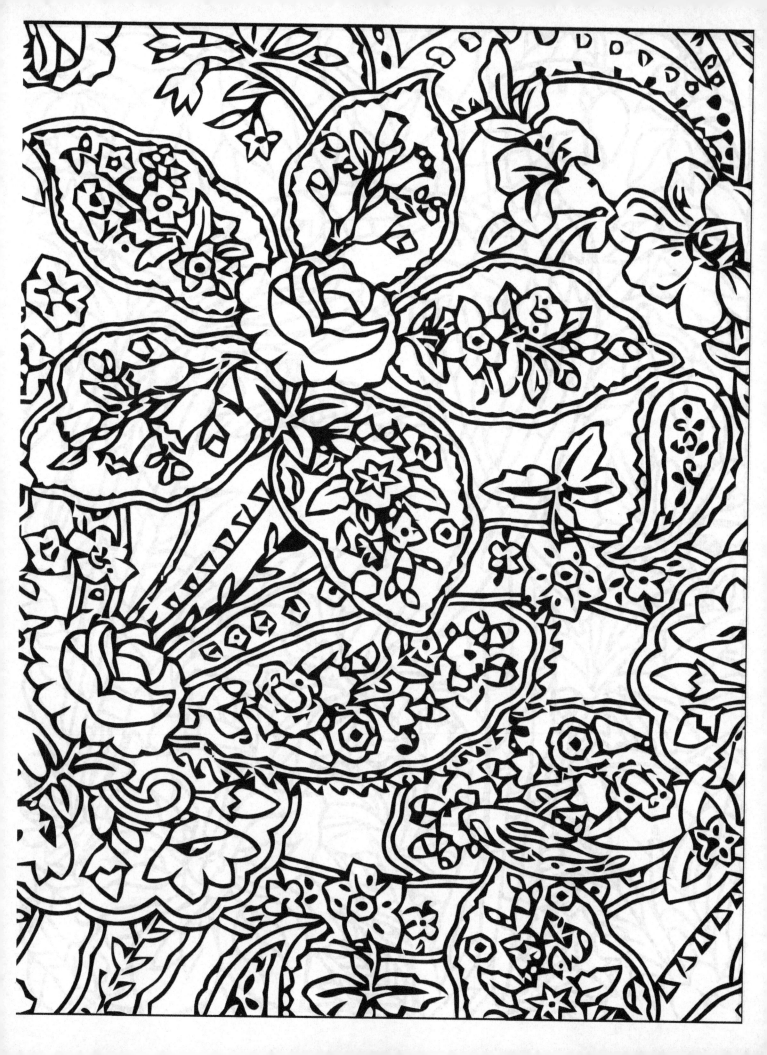

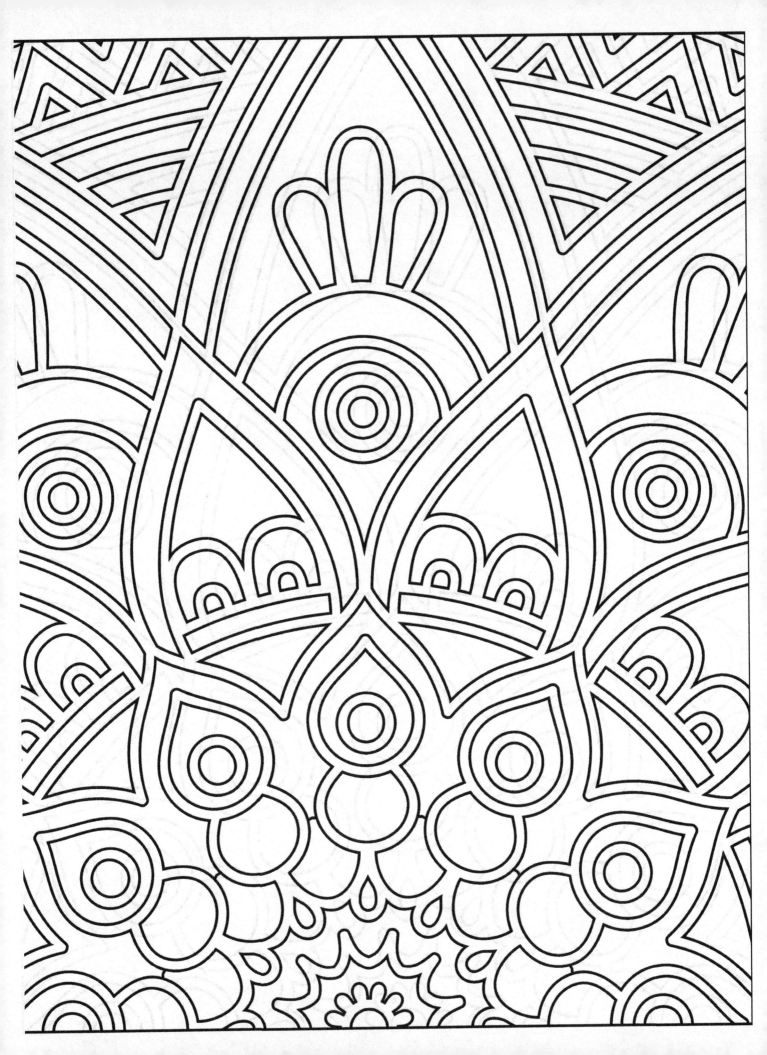

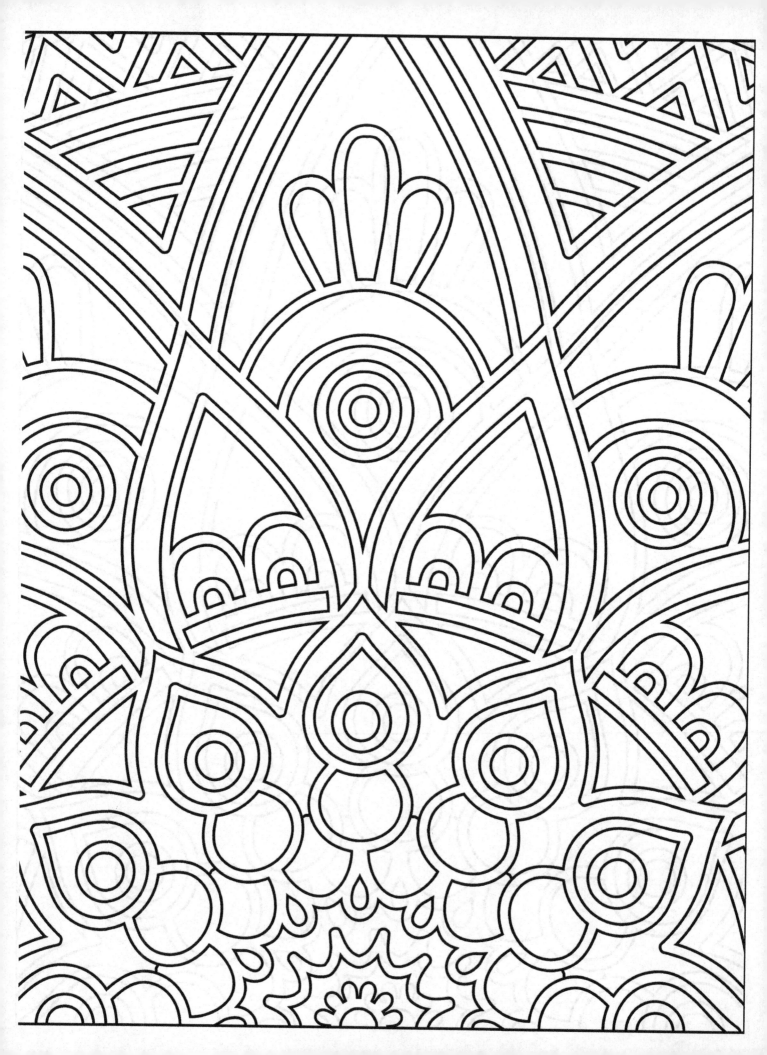

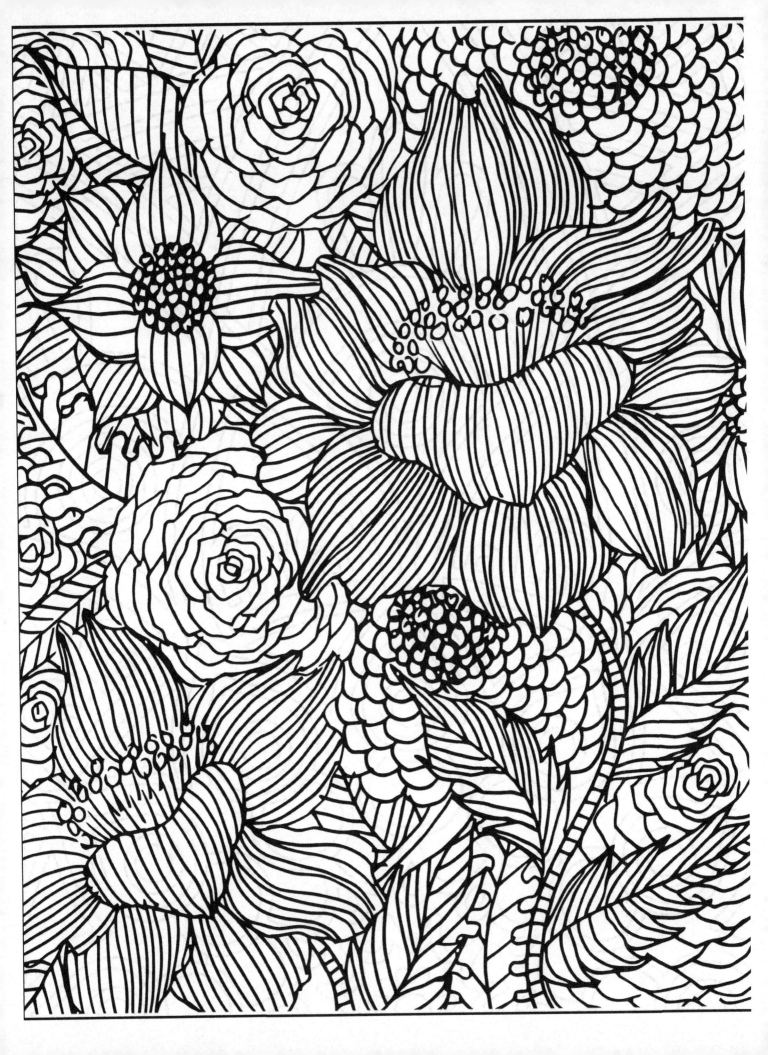

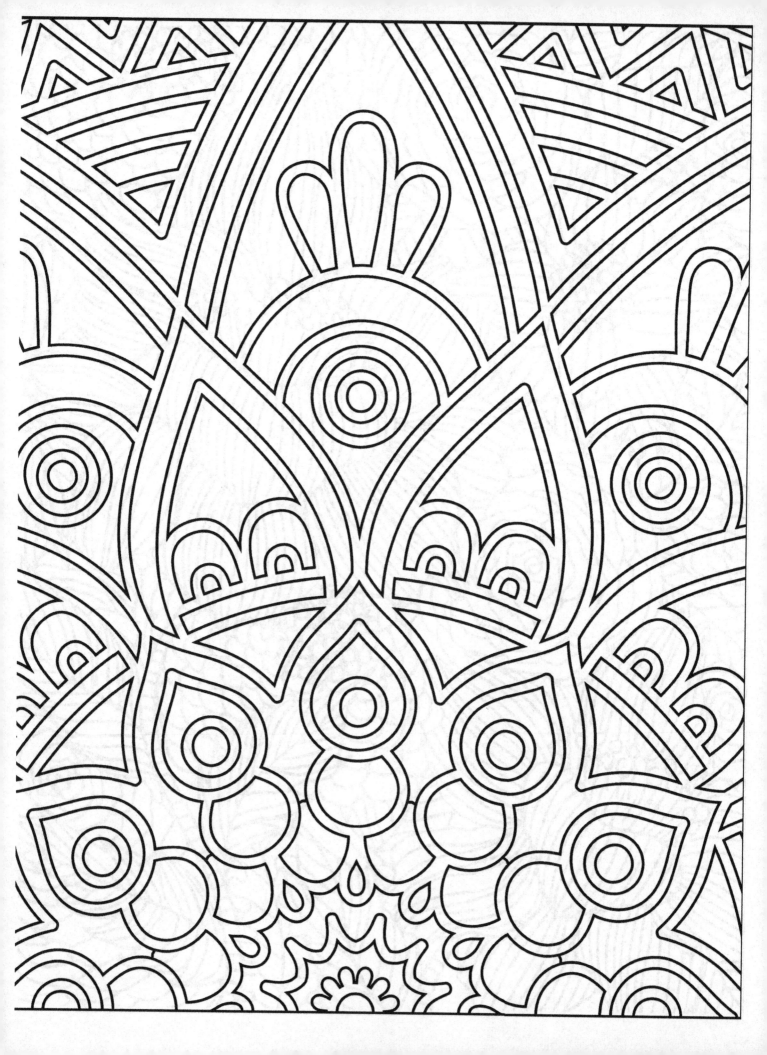

Made in the USA
Columbia, SC
18 December 2024